Fabergé

Fabergé

Court Jeweler to the Tsars

G. von Habsburg-Lothringen

A. von Solodkoff

RIZZOLI
NEW YORK

English translation: J. A. Underwood

Copyright © 1979 Office du Livre, Fribourg, Switzerland

English edition published 1979
in the United States of America by:

RIZZOLI INTERNATIONAL PUBLICATIONS, INC.
712 Fifth Avenue/New York 10019

Library of Congress Catalog Card Number: 79-64335
ISBN 0-8478-0244-2

Printed in Switzerland

Contents

Foreword

No goldsmith of our century has claimed the attention of so many writers as the subject of this book. This has been especially true during the last ten years or so when a plethora of articles in magazines, some scholarly and others merely chic, has been offered to a wide readership in Europe and America. This varied public has displayed an insatiable interest in the products of the Fabergé workshops.

We are entitled to ask ourselves why this particular designer working in Russia at the turn of the century has cast an almost hypnotic spell over so many people all over the world. Having examined a great deal of this material over a number of years, I should like to put forward the following answers.

In the first place we have to recognize the restless curiosity that fired Fabergé's imagination—his probing interest in the history of the applied arts. His enquiring nature by no means confined itself to art history alone, but extended forward, as is so eloquently demonstrated in the pages which follow, to the creation of objects for his own time which have served as models for goldsmiths, enamellers and jewellers ever since.

The second element in his success can surely be attributed to the meticulous quality of every single item which bore the House name; we know that if an object fell below the exacting standard he demanded, that object was never permitted to leave the workshop. This rigorous discipline in itself understandably arouses in us an envy and a sense of nostalgia for a period so very different from our own.

The last quality which I believe accounts for the continuing acclaim for his work is the unconcealed wish to transmit a feeling of goodwill evidentin even the most modest pieces. A tiny enamelled miniature photograph frame, a contented frog carved in nephrite and set with sparkling rose-diamond eyes, a Spring flower in a rock-crystal pot—every one of these objects was planned, not to impress by its magnificence or its cost, but with the uncomplicated aim of giving pleasure to the recipient.

Indeed the history of Fabergé's enterprise is inextricably bound in with the history of making gifts. He conjured up a highly personal anthology of delectable confections designed to serve as the elegant accoutrements for a living society; they were never intended to be imprisoned behind the plate glass of museum vitrines.

It is easy to forget that part of this society was indeed very much alive to new ideas and encouraged artistic endeavour. How appropriate for the authors of this book to discuss in such fascinating detail the *Mir Iskusstva* 'World of Art' movement founded in 1898, which grew around its own eponymous magazine and which brought together many of the most talented artists, theatrical designers and writers working in Russia.

It hardly seems necessary to expatiate here upon the long Habsburg tradition of collecting works of art—all that needs to be set down is that the appreciation for and curiosity about these matters has descended down the line in a highly developed and scholarly form in the amiable person of the Archduke Geza. He has a proved talent for identifying, stalking and hunting down his chosen objective, whether it be a Highland stag or a miniature sedan-chair by Fabergé. His collaborator, Alexander von

Solodkoff, is similarly blessed with a questing mind which does not willingly abandon a seemingly intractible problem, rather does he renew his grip upon it until, by dint of concentrated research, a solution is found.

Their interest has grown as the auction sales of Russian objects they organize for Christie's in Geneva have themselves increased in importance. Their activities, while thoroughly businesslike and extremely successful, have been mercifully free of an exclusively banking approach in spite of the alpine seat of their operations. Indeed the informal atmosphere pervading these well-attended sales is undoubtedly due to their director, rather as a successful party may be credited to the personality of the host.

The writers of this valuable work (which I readily confess I could not put down until I had reached the last page) are to be congratulated upon finding so many relevant facts which have never before been published in a field which has already been diligently worked over by so many others before them.

The discovery of two of the firm's sales ledgers from the London branch in use from 1907 to 1917 is not only exciting in itself, but provides much new and welcome evidence relating to the actual cost and selling prices of objects in stock at that time.

The quality of production of this book is happily on a par with the objects which are illustrated and analysed within its covers.

The authors have presented their scrupulously documented material in the broader context of the decorative arts of the period and their scientific approach to their subject has brought us the readers a rich harvest which leaves us much in their debt.

A. Kenneth Snowman

Preface

This book is not meant to replace the fascinating biography by H. C. Bainbridge, who personally knew Fabergé and was in charge of sales in Fabergé's London branch between 1907 and 1915; nor can it ever lessen the merit of the pioneering work on the art of Fabergé by A. K. Snowman, who was still able to check all his information with Fabergé's children. Rather have the authors sought here to give a full picture of Fabergé's life, based on traditional sources and enriched by new material—unearthed through contacts with the remaining members of the Fabergé family and all the leading specialists in the field, through the reading of Russian sources and a highly informative trip to Leningrad—leading to a fresh assessment of Fabergé's art in the context of his period and in the light of contemporary art movements in Russia. Other new aspects are the analysis of Fabergé's market during his lifetime and up until the present, the discussion of the role of dealers and collectors in connection with Fabergé's art and, for the first time, an insight into the ever-growing world of fakes. Furthermore, all the hallmarks to be found on Fabergé's works are illustrated, and there is a photographic appendix, showing all the known Easter eggs he produced.

The authors have tried to keep off the beaten tracks as far as photographic material is concerned: a large number of the documents used are from the archives of Christie's, Geneva, and many private collectors must be thanked for having made unpublished photographs available. All the major works have been previously illustrated, however inadequately: in many cases new photographs of these were taken for this book.

The authors' special thanks go to A. K. Snowman, London, for his continued help, advice and information over many years; to Léon Grinberg, Paris, the doyen among specialists on Russian art and to Henrik Bolin, Stockholm, the last of the great jewellers still born in Russia. Each of the latter provided a fascinating insight into cultural life in Russia during Fabergé's lifetime and into developments following his death.

Madame Tatiana Fabergé, the widow of Fabergé's grandson Théo, her daughter Tatiana and Igor Fabergé, the master's last living grandson, all helpfully delved into the family archives and came up with unexpected treasures for which they must be especially thanked.

Many leading specialists, collectors and museums have been extremely helpful with information and photographs. The authors would like to thank especially: H.R.H. Princess Eugénie of Greece, Countess Diane de Castellane, Mrs M.M. Postnikova-Loseva (Historic Museum, Moscow), Mrs G. N. Komelova (the Hermitage Museum, Leningrad), Miss Jessie McNab (The Metropolitan Museum, New York), Madame Gilberte Gautier (Cartier, Paris), Dr Armand Hammer (New York), Mr Christopher Forbes (The Forbes Collection, New York), Mr Geoffrey de Bellaigue and Mrs Julie Harland (Lord Chamberlain's Office, London), Mr Urwick Smith (The Wernher Collection, Luton Hoo), Mr and Mrs Harold H. Stream III and Mr Norbert Raake (The Matilda Geddings Grey Foundation, New Orleans), Mr Jacques Kugel (Paris), and Messrs Fensmark Becker (Copenhagen), Mr Bernhard Magaliff (Stockholm), Mr Peter Schaffer (New York), Mr J.S. Sheldon (London), Mr Gabriel Tortella (Geneva) and Mr Emil Kurz (Cologne).

The Family and the Development of the Firm

The Fabergé family can be traced back to the 17th century. It is now accepted that the original name was Favri or Fabri, that the family lived in Picardy in north-east France, and that its members were Huguenots[1].

When Louis XIV revoked the Edict of Nantes in 1685, thus depriving protestants of the right to practise their religion, the Favri, along with so many other Huguenot families, had no alternative but to leave France. The Huguenots sought and found asylum in the protestant states of Switzerland, the Netherlands, Germany, and England, where the majority of them quickly earned the reputation of being skilful and industrious craftsmen. The ancestors of the Fabergés emigrated to Germany and settled in Schwedt, a town on the Oder River north-east of Berlin, changing their name to Favrier or Fabriger.

By the beginning of the 18th century Russia, as a result of the reforms introduced by Peter the Great, had become a country in which craftsmen, artists, and scientists were much in demand, enjoyed enormous success, and often managed to amass considerable fortunes. Moreover since the reign of Catherine II freedom of religion had been enshrined in law. All this made the country extremely attractive to people like Peter Fabergé, a descendant of the original Huguenot family, who in 1800 settled in Pernau in the Baltic province of Livonia and took Russian citizenship. It was here that Gustav Fabergé, Carl's father, was born in 1814.

The young Gustav Fabergé went to St. Petersburg, where he first learnt the goldsmith's art under Master Andreas Ferdinand Spiegel and subsequently entered the well-known firm of Keibel, which in 1826 had reworked the Russian crown jewels.

In 1842 he set up in business on his own (Plate 5), opening a silver and jewellery shop in Bolshaya Morskaya Street—the foundation stone, as it were, of the great House of Fabergé.

Meanwhile Gustav had married Charlotte Jungstedt, the daughter of a Danish painter. On 30 May 1846 Peter Carl Fabergé, better known as Carl (and according to Russian usage as Karl Gustavovitch), was born, the man who was to become the most famous goldsmith of his period.

At the basis of Carl's career lay a sound and extremely wide-ranging education that began at the St. Anne's School (the German-language grammar school in St. Petersburg) and continued in his father's business. This was now so successful that it had become necessary to add the master goldsmith Tsayantkovski to the small staff; at the same time the firm's growing prosperity meant that young Carl was able to complete his education abroad.

In 1860 Gustav Fabergé retired and moved to Dresden, leaving the business in the hands of his managing director and partner, Peter Hiskias Pendin, who also took over the subsequent artistic training of Gustav's son. Meanwhile Carl had joined his father in Dresden and later entered an apprenticeship with the jeweller Friedmann in Frankfurt am Main, where he also began to study economics. After study trips to England and Italy he completed his business training in Paris, so complementing his artistic training with a solid grounding in commercial affairs.

In 1870, at the age of twenty-four, Carl returned to St. Petersburg and took over the management of the family firm. In 1872 he married Augusta Julia Jakobs, whose father was overseer in the imperial furniture workshops. The couple had four sons: Eugène, who was born in 1874, Agathon, born in 1876, and Alexander and Nicholas, born in 1877 and 1884 respectively. All four were subsequently to work for the firm.

Carl Fabergé moved the firm out of his father's rather small jewellery shop into very much larger premises, also in Bolshaya Morskaya Street (Plate 7), which together with the Nevsky Prospect was one of the two main commercial thoroughfares of St. Petersburg. Here it became clear that, on top of his out-standing artistic gifts, Carl also possessed a great talent for organization, building up his firm, which he ran in collaboration with several partners until 1903, into a big business in the modern sense. The success of the House of Fabergé was a typical example of the technical and economic boom that Russia enjoyed in the latter half of the 19th century.

Fabergé's novel idea of manufacturing *objects de fantaisie* (the product of an artist-craftsman's imagination, resulting in a small object having both artistic and functional value) was so successful that he was positively swamped with commissions. In order to meet the demand the firm was continually having to increase its staff, so that in 1900 a further, final move became necessary, this time to a new building at 24 Bolshaya Morskaya Street, and between 1907–17 Fabergé employed up to 700 people—master goldsmiths and craftsmen—in St. Petersburg and in his branches elsewhere in Russia. Workshops and shops were opened in Moscow in 1887, in Odessa in 1890, and in Kiev in 1905. With the business grown to such proportions it is understandable that Fabergé's main job was not so much on the actual manufacturing side as in organization and management. This also explains why no piece can be proven to have come from Fabergé's own hand.

The history of the firm was marked, as far as the outside world was concerned, by the award of the title 'Supplier to the Imperial Court' in 1884. This was connected with the completion in that year of the first imperial Easter egg (Cat. Plate 1) for Tsar Alexander III, evidently to the tsar's entire satisfaction. Tsar Nicholas II continued his father's custom of ordering his presents for special occasions from Fabergé. After an exhibition of Fabergé objects in the palace of Grand Duke Vladimir Alexandrovich in 1902, his pieces—replicas of the crown jewels (Plate 17)—were by imperial permission put on show in the Hermitage. In addition to the influential imperial family, Fabergé soon numbered members of the wealthy Russian aristocracy and bourgeoisie among his clients, from Prince Youssoupov and Count Stroganoff to the Nobel brothers, the gold-mining magnate Kelch, and the rubber manufacturer Neuscheller.

Meanwhile the name of Fabergé as a synonym for goldsmith's work of outstanding quality had spread from Russia throughout Western Europe and even to America. In 1885 Fabergé received the gold medal of the Nuremberg Exhibition for his copies—exhibited there—of the Scythian gold treasures. In 1897, on the occasion of the Nordic Exhibition in Stockholm, he was appointed 'Goldsmith to the Court of the King of Sweden and Norway'. A high-point in the history of the firm was the 1900 World Exhibition in Paris where, at the express wish of Tsarina Alexandra, Fabergé's imperial Easter presents received their first public showing, *hors concours*.

1 Portrait bust of Carl Fabergé by Joseph Limburg, 1903.

2 Carl Fabergé sorting a parcel of loose stones, photographed by Hugo Oeberg.

3 Fabergé in Pully, Switzerland, in July, 1920, two months before his death.

4 Profile portrait of Carl Fabergé. (Unpublished original photograph from the Fabergé family archives.)

5 Diamond-set gold bangle by Gustave Fabergé in the original fitted case. One of the rare recorded pieces made by Carl Fabergé's father.

6 Cover of the 1899 catalogue of the Moscow branch of the House of Fabergé, advertising diamonds, gold and silverware.

7 View of Fabergé's premises at 24 Bolshaya Morskaya Street, St. Petersburg.

8 View of Fabergé's Moscow premises. In contrast to the discreet outer appearance of the St. Petersburg business, the Moscow shop loudly advertised its name and imperial warrant.

9–12 Interiors of Fabergé workshops. It is interesting to note how young some of the workmen were, e. g. Pl. 10. In Pl. 11 the Chanticleer Egg of 1904 (see Pl. 143) can be seen on the workbench.

5

6

7

8

9

10

11

12

13

14

15

16

They astonished the jury: Fabergé was unanimously made a master of the Parisian Goldsmiths' Guild and was presented in addition with the Cross of the Legion of Honour[2].

In 1903 Fabergé opened what was to be his only foreign branch—in London. He had a number of enthusiastic supporters in the English royal family, notably Queen Alexandra, who had probably been introduced to his work by her sister, the Russian Tsarina Maria Feodorovna.

Eventually Fabergé's fame spread to the Far East, and in 1904 he received an invitation to visit the court of King Maha Chulalongkorn of Siam, for whom Fabergé made a number of pieces—many of them in nephrite—which are still in the Thai royal family's collection.

The First World War put an end to the activities of the House of Fabergé as to so much else: the London branch had to close in 1915: the budget for imperial commissions was drastically curtailed. In 1914 the workshops were ordered to start producing small arms for the front and dressing material for the wounded; cigarette cases and ashtrays were made of gunmetal or of copper to comply with wartime economies and only decorated with the Russian eagle and the inscription '1914 War'.

Following the October Revolution 1917 a 'Committee of the Employees of the Cooperative K. Fabergé' was formed, which took over the management of the firm until late 1918, when Fabergé emigrated.

In September 1918, under the protection of a foreign ambassador, Carl Fabergé and his family left Russia, stopping at Riga and Berlin before settling in Wiesbaden, Germany. In 1920, Fabergé and his wife moved into the Hotel Bellevue in Lausanne, Switzerland (Plate 3), where he died on 24 September of the same year. His family had his body, along with that of his wife Charlotte (who had died in 1925) moved to Cannes in southern France in 1929.

The Foundation of Fabergé's Success

The astonishing success of the House of Fabergé arose out of Carl's own idea of combining embellished *objets d'art* (small objects of artistic value), and functional objects into what he called *'objets de fantaisie'*, an idea that first came to fruition in the firm around 1884 with the creation of the original imperial Easter egg[3].

The applied arts of the period in Europe from 1860 to about 1908 were characterized by a sumptuousness that took its cue from the baroque, from the Napoleon III-style to art nouveau. A common type of jewellery in that period was the bouquet of flowers heavily encrusted with diamonds; typical decorative objects were magnificent centrepieces with elaborate allegorical figures. The usual jewellery boxes, with their flowing lines, were decorated, if not with diamonds, at least with paste. This clear tendency towards luxurious display in the applied arts should be seen against the background of the industrial transformation that Europe was undergoing at the time. It also led to a general climate of prosperity, to which the arts responded by producing a new wealth of forms.

From about the middle of the 1880s, however, the applied arts found the ability to develop a more subtle relationship to ornament in the broadest sense. Their function ceased to be that of simply parading evidence of prosperity, and a certain refinement of form began to emerge. Tastes had changed, and people now wanted their ornamental objects to be as restrained as possible; the decoratively ostentatious piece of jewellery was regarded as inelegant.

Fabergé's *objets de fantaisie* were perfectly in tune with the requirements of this new taste. He was concerned with the visual impression created by a piece, without regard to the value of the materials used. What distinguishes his work from that of his predecessors and most contemporaries is the fact that it avoids the showy use of costly materials such as large diamonds and precious stones; preferring relatively inexpensive semiprecious stones or tiny rose diamonds in the place of large areas of polished precious metals, he used enamels of unprecedented colourfulness and multicoloured gold. The combination of these materials with workmanship of the highest precision gave to Fabergé objects not the kind of extravagance that impresses at first sight but a refinement that can be fully appreciated only on closer examination. This is particularly true of the practical wares that Fabergé produced in such a variety of shapes—cigarette cases, vanity cases, notebooks, perfume flasks, bonbonnières, writing equipment, umbrella handles, bell pushes, and so on.

Moreover such a Fabergé piece had an additional attraction: in using it the owner was himself displaying a certain elegance of style. This kind of association gradually made Fabergé objects synonymous with a fashionable, sophisticated life-style, a trend that was not inhibited by the fact that Fabergé was jeweller by appointment to nearly all the ruling houses of Europe; in other words to the very people looked up to by society at that time. It became chic to shop at Fabergé and to be seen with examples of his work or to give them as presents.

Fabergé sought to meet this tremendous demand by increasing his staff on the one hand and, on the other, by drawing upon the apparently unlimited resources of his

17 Miniatura replica of the Russian imperial regalia in platinum and diamonds. Made for the 1900 World Fair in Paris, the regalia were shown there alongside the imperial Easter eggs and afterwards displayed in the Hermitage (Leningrad), where they still are today. The tsar's crown is 7 cm high; the tsarina's crown 3.5 cm high and the sceptre 14.5 cm high. There is an engraved Cyrillic signature and date on the silver base: K. Fabergé SPB 1900. The regalia were probably made in A. Holmström's workshop, although the base is by workmaster J. Rappoport.

18 Imperial presentation snuffbox of enamelled gold with a portrait of Tsar Alexander III, presented by him to Prince Otto von Bismarck.

19 Silver-mounted frame made of palisander with a photograph of Tsar Nicholas II in the uniform of a German admiral, 42.5 cm high, workmaster Anders Nevalainen. Presnted to vice-admiral Albert von Seckendorff during the tsar's visit to Kiel in 1909.

20 Informal photograph of Tsar Nicholas II at his desk; on it are a number of frames (some of which are by Fabergé), containing photographs of members of the imperial family. Probably taken c. 1910 in a palace outside St. Petersburg.

21–22 Closed and open views of a heart-shaped triple frame of enamelled gold, set with gems; Pl. 22 shows the portraits that it contains: Tsar Nicholas II, his wife Alexandra Feodorovna and their second daughter Tatiana. The exterior is in red guilloché enamel, 8.4 cm high, signed with Fabergé's engraved signature (found only on imperial commissions) and dated 1897. (The Forbes Collection, New York).

17

18

19

20

23

24

imagination. The supply of functional wares and *objets de vitrine* (small objects for display) in ever-changing designs was further enriched by the breadth of his enamellers' palette. Fabergé encouraged constant experimentation to find fresh nuances of enamel colour for his objects. Certain shades met with a particularly enthusiastic reception. In Edwardian London, for example, it was the pieces in raspberry-red enamel, in Paris those in opalescent pink that, for a while, charmed Fabergé's clients. Often a vanity case or a powder compact in a particularly successful shade of enamel would, needless to say, serve as a pretext for having an entire ball gown made in a matching material.

A contributory factor in Fabergé's success was the way in which his objects embraced modern technological developments. Towards the end of the 19th century the art of portraiture was revolutionized by the widespread introduction of photography. Photographs began to take the place of painted portraits and miniatures, and such was the public enthusiasm for the new art form that by the turn of the century it had become common practice to exhibit a row of photographs of friends and the members of one's family on a desk or on top of a cabinet. The photographs needed frames, and this offered Fabergé enormous scope for the manufacture of decorative objects using a wide variety of materials and techniques.

In the same way Fabergé exploited another domestic novelty—the electric table bell, which was replacing the hand bell as the means of summoning servants. An ornamental bell push not only constituted a focal point in an interior but also testified to the affluence of the household.

As well as producing pieces based on his own ideas, Fabergé sometimes worked to specific commissions. Examples of this type of work are the copies of the Scythian Treasure made for Count Sergej Stroganoff, president of the Imperial Archeological Commission, as well as various objects Fabergé made in the blue-and-yellow colours of Léopold de Rothshild's racing stable (Plate 152) and the brooches featuring the Russian crown that the Tsarina Alexandra Feodorovna designed and gave to her ladies-in-waiting on the occasion of the birth of the heir to the Russian throne in 1904.

In discussing such a commission with a client, Fabergé was particularly good both at recognizing exactly what was wanted and at using his artistic and technical experience to turn the wish into reality. He acted as mediator between what was technically possible and what the client had in mind, with the result that his pieces reflect very closely the taste of his period. This also accounts for the heterogeneous nature of his work, since he sought to appeal to as many clients as possible. In fact his approach of serving the client's needs first, shows clearly how Fabergé saw himself: not as an artist in his own right but as the leader and co-ordinator of a body of outstanding artist-craftsmen.

The shop in St. Petersburg's Bolshaya Morskaya Street became a place of pilgrimage for more than just Russian society. The majority of visitors from abroad also called at the House of Fabergé to admire the latest creations, a rich assortment of which was permanently on display in the firm's spacious salerooms (Plate 16). Both to keep pace with the broad spectrum of demand and at the same time to demonstrate the range of his abilities, Fabergé liked to keep in stock at all times a selection of pieces as varied as possible.

While the St. Petersburg clientèle was made up of the Russian aristocracy and foreigners, the Moscow branch (Plate 8) catered mainly to the wealthy business commun-

23   Table clock of silver-gilt and scarlet guilloché enamel over a sunburst pattern with applied crossed arrows, 9 cm wide, workmaster Michael Perchin.
Brush pot of silver-gilt and scarlet guilloché enamel over a wave pattern with applied laurel swags, 8.7 cm high, workmaster Anders Nevalainen.

24   Oval silver frame with red guilloché enamel and applied varicoloured swags, 7.8 cm high, signed, workmaster Victor Aarne, 1899–1908 (no. 5191).
Tcharka (vodka cup) of gold and red enamel; the handle is set with a half-rouble of Tsarina Elizabeth that is enamelled in red and surrounded by rose-diamonds, 5.2 cm high, signed, workmaster Michael Perchin, before 1899.
Heart-shaped frame of silver-gilt and red enamel with applied varicoloured swags, 7.2 cm high, signed, workmaster Victor Aarne, before 1899 (no. 1119).

ity in that city. The kings and emperors who had granted Fabergé the privilege of an appointment to their courts, however, rarely appeared themselves in his sale rooms. They would invite Fabergé or one of his sons to bring a selection of objects for a private viewing and to discuss future commissions. The imperial court in St. Petersburg required such quantities of Fabergé articles—not just for private gifts within the family (Plate 20), but principally as official presents for important persons both at home and abroad (Plate 18)—that a special room in the Winter Palace was set aside for the purpose and stocked with suitable pieces. Here the palace official responsible for state gifts (N. N. Novosselsky was the last to hold this position.), or on rare occasions the tsar himself, would choose the most appropriate piece for each occasion. Once a month Eugèene Fabergé came to check what had been taken in order to prepare the invoices and stock up again with new pieces.

In addition to exhibitions on the firm's premises and others that were held by private arrangement, Fabergé published illustrated catalogues (Plate 6), the introductions to which are especially informative as regards conditions of sale[4]. Basically these catalogues were designed for clients who, 'because they live in the provinces, have no opportunity of visiting our premises personally and of seeing for themselves our rich selection of goods'.

The note on prices contained in them, however, can be taken to apply to everything the firm produced: this catalogue note pointed out that all articles were sold at as low a price as their meticulous workmanship allowed; moreover, they carried with them the firm's guarantee to take back or exchange individual pieces provided that these had not been made to order, that they were not damaged, and that they had been purchased fairly recently[5]. It is interesting that the firm's wide range of models and designs was matched by a wide range of prices (see Fabergé's Market and Prices). In the 1899 catalogue, for example, we read: 'Taking account both the needs of the higher classes of society as well as the interests of the middle class, we provide both the luxury and expensive goods to satisfy the most refined taste as well as the unexpensive goods within the reach of the not too well-to-do'.

The Fabergé Style

The Fabergé style can be described as a combination of heterogeneous elements that, taken as a whole, does not fit easily into any of the stylistic categories put forward by art critics and historians. The style can no more be regarded as wholly eclectic in character than can Fabergé be classified as an exponent of art nouveau, nor can it be called either purely French or purely Russian. The majority of the work, however, is at least associated with eclecticism in so far as it makes use of historical styles; for the eclectic trend known as historicism had been current in art since the middle of the 19th century. It sought to borrow and imitate art forms from history and reproduce them in refined and reworked forms. Typical examples of the trend were the re-use of gothic, and later renaissance, then baroque stylistic features, the last in conjunction with rococo elements (Plate 30 and 47). Historicism had just worked round to adopting the Louis XVI style when it was eclipsed, around 1895, by the rise of art nouveau, the 'modern style' that represented a fresh approach to art and a turning away from established historical forms.

Fabergé made particular use of renaissance and baroque art forms. The foundations for his virtuoso exploitation of these styles had been laid during his years of study in Dresden and Florence.

As a young man Fabergé had studied the collections in Dresden's *Grünes Gewölbe*, (Green Vaults) Collection, included 16th-century *Kunstkammer* objects, (a connoisseur's collection of curiosities and works of art), Renaissance enamelled jewellery, Saxon gem-carving work, and 18th-century pieces by Johann Melchior Dinglinger and by Neuber. Here was one of the sources not only of Fabergé's inexhaustible supply of artistic ideas but also of the perfectionism that, inspired by the high standards of the earlier goldsmiths, he brought to his own work. The visits to Florence for his studies exerted a similar influence. There it was the collection of the Palazzo Pitti with its figures and reliefs in polychrome marble and semiprecious stones from the *Opificio delle Pietre Dure* (Medici hardstone-carving factory) and its hardstone vessels and enamels from the time of the Florentine Renaissance that caught the young man's imagination and the gothic element in many of Fabergé's pieces stemmed from his apprenticeship years in Frankfurt.

A constant source of influence, and one far nearer to Fabergé, was the Treasury of the Hermitage, where works of art mainly of the 18th century had been hoarded by Russia's tsars. Major works by the goldsmiths of Paris and Berlin, and by the lapidaries of Dresden and Florence fill the showcases of the Treasure House, including many objects by Russian goldsmiths and jewellers of the late 18th century (Plate 120). It may safely be assumed that Fabergé not only knew the Hermitage from his early years but also had constant access to it as jeweller to the Court.

The work Fabergé produced in the gothic, renaissance, and baroque styles was within the mainstream of historicism as practised throughout Europe. Subsequently, however, he extended historicism to include both the Louis XVI and Empire styles. The Empire style went down particularly well in Russia , since it called to mind the heroic era of the Russian victory over Napoleon and the Wars of Liberation. (In 1912, for the 100th anniversary, there were special celebrations throughout Russia).[6]

The later output of the Fabergé workshops was characterized by extensive use of the more severe Louis XVI and Empire styles (Plate 32) as opposed to the exuberance of art nouveau. This gave Fabergé's work as a whole a courtly, traditional orientation that, of course, was in harmony with the political outlook of the conservative ruling classes, who to a greater or lesser extent rejected art nouveau. In this respect there is a real temptation to see the art of Fabergé as an expression of conservatism as against the general background of historicism.

In imitating each historical style Fabergé took as his model original pieces that he had come across on his travels. In some cases he commissioned copies of objects in private collections; in other cases he purchased originals himself—for example the gold boxes he bought in Paris—in order to manufacture replicas or study more closely their style and workmanship. Copying was always only the first step in the process of redeploying the stylistic elements concerned in new combinations and for novel uses; Fabergé was at least never guilty of the stereotyped application of historical ornaments.

In obedience to contemporary taste and the demands of his international clientèle, Fabergé did of course also produce work in the art-nouveau idiom (Plates 34 and 35), though the chief exponent of this style in jewellery was Lalique. Fabergé's attitude to art nouveau, the so-called 'modern style', appears to have been somewhat ambivalent. Art nouveau—or *Jugendstil,* as it was called in the German-speaking world —reacted against the imitation of historical styles by taking the vegetable kingdom as the basis for ornamental work. According to the use they made of plant forms, the exponents of art nouveau can be divided into two groups: those who confined themselves to a naturalistic approach, and those who went on to develop abstract forms based on plant rhythms. Articles using the latter approach are relatively rare in Fabergé's work and consist in the main of objects such as table silver, small pieces of jewellery, and boxes; they are almost invariably of silver, occasionally gilt, and come mainly from the Moscow workshop (Plate 34).

But if he produced few interesting examples of abstract art nouveau, Fabergé could be described as one of the early pioneers of the naturalistic school of applied art: his flowers (Plates 109–112) in semiprecious stones and enamel are impressive precisely because of their naturalism, an effect that is enhanced by the fact that, with very few exceptions, only a single spray is represented in each case. This purely naturalistic approach, eschewing all symbolism, was something new in the art of the turn of the century and attracted a certain amount of criticism from contemporaries on the grounds that the flowers were more like a coloured photograph and as such hardly capable of conveying a tastefully artistic impression.[7] Fabergé's individual flower sprays are reminiscent of the floral still-lifes so common in Far-Eastern art (Plate 111), for example ink drawings, lacquer work, and ceramics from China and Japan. These parallels are quite understandable in the context of art nouveau, which found one of its major sources of inspiration in the Japanese prints that Europe imported in increasing quantities from the mid 1880s onwards. The fact that it turned goldsmiths back towards the plant world as their primary source of inspiration was regarded as one of the triumphs of Japanese influence.[8]

25 Oval bowl made of jasper; the gold dragon-shaped handle is decorated with cabochon sapphires and has ruby eyes, 17.5 cm long, workmaster Erik Kollin.

26 Two-handled cup of smoky quartz, gold-mounted, in the Renaissance style, 5.7 cm high, workmaster Erik Kollin—a good example of his archaic style.

27 Silver-gilt *Scherzbecher,* shaped as a figure playing the bagpipes, 23 cm high, signed, workmaster Julius Rappoport, 1899–1908. This is a copy after a similar 17th-century German figure in silver in the Armoury Museum, Moscow.

28 Silver box in the 17th-century German style; the gadrooned lid is set with a silver-gilt medal of Duke Rudolph August of Braunschweig-Lüneburg dated 1683, 10.8 cm across, signed, workmaster Julius Rappoport.

29 *Kovsh* (ladle-shaped drinking vessel) of silver-gilt and cloisonné enamel, 13 cm long, imperial warrant mark, Moscow 1899–1908.

30 Rectangular dish of nephrite with gold handles in the rococo style, set with gems. The handles are enamelled in red and set with rose-diamonds, 37 cm long, signed, workmaster Henrik Wigström.

31 Fan-shaped triple photograph frame of silver-gilt in red guilloché enamel, decorated with Louis-XV scrolls, 9 cm high, workmaster Michael Perchin.

27

28

29

30

31

Fabergé himself was extremely interested in Japanese art and built up his own collection of *netsukes* (carved toggles), which eventually numbered some 500 items.[9] He made some straight copies of *netsuke* figures, but quite apart from that his own naturalistic animal figures showed the influence of these art objects from Japan. Another source of ideas can be recognized in Meissen porcelain animals of which Fabergé possessed quite a collection.[10]

Certain Fabergé articles are so totally original in shape and design that we can detect in them neither historicist nor art-nouveau influences; their style is truly modern. This applies particularly to the practical objects that, dispensing entirely with artistic ornamentation, embody the notion of practical utility in its purest form. Prime examples of this are the cigarette cases (Plates 62 an 63) in completely smooth or ribbed gold set only with a cabochon (less for decorative purposes than to serve as a thumb-piece to open the case). In addition to these 'Fabergé-design' cigarette cases, which became famous and are still widely imitated today, Fabergé also manufactured powder compacts and pillboxes (Plates 98 an 99). The same sort of clear, purely utilitarian shapes occur in some of his tea and coffee sevices, where the art of the 1920s seems foreshadowed.[11]

The elements of Fabergé's style that we have described so far—those emerging from historicism and art nouveau—all enjoyed international currency. But what kinds of Russian influence did Fabergé allow to enter his work?

The fact that Fabergé was of French extraction has often led people to overemphasize the French stylistic elements in his work or even to classify him purely and simply as a French artist. Fabergé, however, is yet another example of the phenomenon that typifies so many of the foreign artists to have worked in Russia during the last three centuries: they all adapted themselves to the circumstances of their adopted country, and ultimately to its sheer physical size, in a way that makes it tempting to speak of a *genius loci*. This found expression in, on the one hand, a certain expansiveness in terms of an emphasis on and blending of stylistic elements and, on the other, in exploitation of the country's wealth of available materials. This also comes out clearly in the work of the artists and craftsmen—mostly of Italian or German extraction—who for several centuries (but more especially since the invitation issued by Peter the Great) had been emigrating to Russia in large numbers.

As far as Fabergé's work is concerned, direct Russian influence can be seen in a series of objects whose shape and purpose alone stamp them as typically Russian. These include the icons (Plate 37), baptismal crosses, and ecclesiastical implements whose basic design derives from artistic traditions developed within the Orthodox church. These partly Byzantine, partly old-Russian designs were often blended by Fabergé with western European stylistic elements. Many of the icon paintings, for example, are done in a mellow, Raphael-like style while their frames (*oklad* or *riza*, rectangular icon frames, usually in silver) show baroque or Empire features.

The custom of giving and receiving symbolic eggs at Easter was very much more widespread in Russia than in western Europe, and this led to another typically Russian product of the Fabergé workshops: the miniature pendant in the shape of an egg (Plate 124), and the large-size Easter eggs made for the tsar (Cat. Plates 1–69).

Fabergé's work also includes a number of objects fashioned after traditional Russian receptacles or shapes; in this Fabergé hardly differed from his competitors. Especially

32 Silver-mounted calender clipboard of cherry-wood in the Empire style, 28 cm high, signed, workmaster Anders Nevalainen, 1899–1908.

33 Gold-mounted bonbonnière in nephrite, shaped as a piano and in the Empire style, 7.5 cm long, signed, workmaster Michael Perchin (no. 5852). It is mentioned in the sales ledger of the London branch of the House of Fabergé as sold to Viscountess Curzon on 28 July, 1913, for £ 62 ($ 300); it had cost 350 roubles to make (£ 35/$ 170). In November, 1977 it was sold at Christie's Geneva for Sfr. 62,000 (£ 13,000/$ 25,000).

popular as decorative objects were the *bratina* (a round punch bowl) (Plate 91) and the *kovsh* (originally a drinking vessel whose ladle-shaped form can be traced back to the Scythians, Plates 39 an 40). In earlier days the *kovsh* had been carved in wood in the form of a duck, with the neck serving as the handle. Over the centuries this naturalistic form grew progressively more abstract, so that examples from the 16th and 17th centuries only vaguely recall the original duck shape. Subsequently the *kovsh* became something more than a simple peasant drinking vessel; made of silver or gold, it served as a sumptuous decorative object that the princes of Moscow and later the tsars awarded to individuals for services rendered (Plate 43). Perhaps the best known examples are those from the 18th century, decorated with the double-headed eagle of the imperial coat-of-arms.

Fabergé's work, too, often features the double-headed eagle as a decorative motif (Plate 91): as the tsar's personal coat-of-arms on articles made for him and on other articles as the national emblem of Russia. Fabergé also made extensive ornamental use of the imperial crown as well as of various military emblems, particularly badges and helmets. A notable feature of many Fabergé pieces is their use of old Russian coins, silver and gold roubles of the period from Peter the Great to Catherine II (Plate 24). The backgrounds of the coins were often given a guilloché finish and then enamelled, so that the sovereign's profile stands out attractively from a coloured enamel surround.

There is another class of articles that Fabergé produced in a Russian style called the Romanov Tercentenary style. Modelled on the art of 17th-century Russia, it was characterized by intertwined vine and arabesque motifs, often in conjunction with the double-headed eagle emblem. This style made its appearance around 1913, the third centenary of the Romanov dynasty's accession to the throne of Russia in 1613. This three-hundredth anniversary was the occasion of sumptuous festivities in the course of which the imperial family distributed numerous official gifts from the Fabergé workshops. The Romanov Tercentenary style, like the firm's cloisonné enamel work, was greeted with approval by those Russians who had no time for the Western fashions predominating in St. Petersburg. Among the ranks of the traditionalists were members of the old *boyar* (Russian title of nobility before Peter the Great) dynasties as well as the wealthy merchant families of Moscow.

What has been calledthe 'Fabergé style' is thus a blend of elements drawn from international movements—historicism and art nouveau—with elements drawn from the Russian national tradition, all of them enhanced and made more effective by the quality and refinement of the firm's workmanship.

The Fabergé style emerged during the formative years of the *Mir Iskusstva* ('World of Art') movement, in the context of which Fabergé's work must be seen. *Mir Iskusstva* was an association of artists and writers, founded in 1898; through its magazine of the same name it played an important part in the development of Russian art in the early years of this century. The central figures of the movement were A. Benois, K. Somov, L. Bakst, E. Lanceray, and S. Diaghilev. The magazine *Mir Iskusstva* gathered round it the same sort of avant-garde artists and writers as *Jugend* did in Munich, *Studio* in London, and the *Revue Blanche* in Paris—further proof of the close ties between literature and the visual arts that characterized the period. The importance of the movement was threefold: it brought life back into the arts, in con-

34 Silver knife and fork in the art-nouveau style, imperial warrant mark, Moscow, 1899–1908.

35 Nephrite bowl on a silver-gilt art-nouveau foot, 21 cm high, signed, workmaster Victor Aarne, St. Petersburg, 1899–1908. It is unusual to find objects in art-nouveau style made in the St. Petersburg workshops.

36 Silver-gilt cream jug of unusual triangular form, 6.5 cm high, Moscow assay mark for 1896, imperial warrant mark (no.6326). This documentary piece foreshadows the functional shapes of the art-deco period in the 1920s.

37 Parcel-gilt icon of St. Paul, 11 cm across, signed, workmaster Michael Perchin.

38 Gold cigarette case with blue enamel bands, 8.5 cm long, signed, workmaster Henrik Wigström.

39 Large silver *kovsh* (ladle-shaped drinking vessel) in the traditional pan-Slavic style; the handle is chased with a 17th-century double-headed eagle, 33 cm long, imperial warrant mark, Moscow, 1908–17.

40 Large rectangular *kovsh* (ladle-shaped drinking vessel) of silver set with cabochons of amethyst and chrysoprase, 34 cm long, signed.

41 Silver samovar on four claw feet, chased with leaf ornaments in the pan-Slavic style, 63 cm high, imperial warrant mark, Moscow, 1899–1908.

34

35

43

42

44

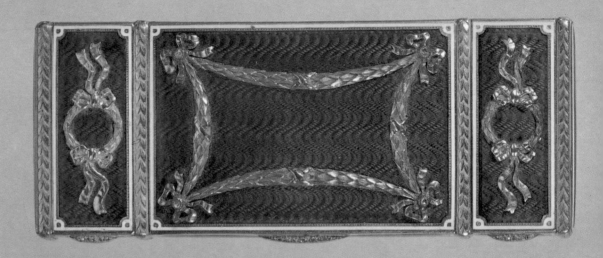

42   Large silver tankard, 29 cm high, signed, workmaster Stephan Wäkevä.

43   Imperial presentation *kovsh* of nephrite; the gold and enamel handle is set with rose-diamonds and the monogram of Tsar Nicholas II, 25 cm long, signed, workmaster Michael Perchin, 1899–1908 (no. 3926). Presented to the French Ambassador in St. Petersburg, M. Boutiron, whose widow gave it to the Musée des Arts Décoratifs in Paris in 1927.

44   Large silver punch bowl shaped as an art-nouveau *kovsh,* 32 cm high, imperial warrant mark, Moscow, 1899–1908.

45   Nephrite tray in the Renaissance style; the gold handles are enamelled in various colours and set with large circular-cut diamonds, 34 cm long, signed, workmaster Michael Perchin. It was presented by the Dutch Colony of St. Petersburg to the Dutch Queen Wilhelmine on the occasion of her wedding in 1901. This one of Fabergé's major pieces and the best example of the Renaissance style in his œuvre.

46   Enamelled lotus-flower vase of nephrite, gold-mounted and set with gems, 25 cm high, signed, workmaster Michael Perchin, 1899–1908.
This is a fine example of the Chinese influence in Fabergé's art. (A la Vieille Russie, New York).

47   Table clock of silver-gilt and green guilloché enamel in the rococo style, 20 cm high, signed, workmaster Michael Perchin. The use of scrolls in this piece is typical of Perchin's predilection for baroque shapes.

48   Gold case of Louis XV design, shaped and enamelled in pearl grey over a guilloché wave pattern; the chased and applied scrolls are set with rose-diamonds, 10.3 cm high, signed, workmaster Michael Perchin, before 1899 (no. 1502).
Oblong vanity case with three compartments, of gold and dark green guilloché enamel, 11 cm long, signed, workmaster Henrik Wigström, 1908–17.
Oblong vanity case of silver-gilt with panels of pearlgrey and white guilloché enamel; the applied swags are of varicoloured gold, 11 cm long, signed, workmaster Henrik Wigström, 1908–17 (no. 22549).

trast to the staid academic tradition of painting; it established links with the rest of European art, particularly with the progressive French movements; and it sought generally to turn St. Petersburg into a Russian artistic centre of international stature. *Mir Iskusstva* succeeded in reviving the artistic and cultural traditions of 18th- and early 19th-century Russia on the one hand and, on the other, in making known in Russia the work of such foreign artists as Cézanne, van Gogh, and Matisse. The movement attached particular importance to bringing together different branches of the arts, for example, in theatrical decor, with Diaghilev's work with the *Ballet Russe.* It also championed the applied arts; for example Somov, who received an award for his pictures at the 1900 World Exhibition in Paris, also designed a famous group of porcelain figures.

The links between Fabergé and the *Mir Iskusstva* movement were extremely close. In particular he was in direct touch with Alexander Benois, whose St. Petersburg correspondence with Eugène and Agathon Fabergé has survived.[12] We also know that Benois, who had made a particular study of baroque and rococo in France and Russia, did designs for Fabergé. The design for the 1905 Colonnade Easter Egg (Plate 129) in the form of a temple with cupids and a revolving clock can be attributed to him.[13]

Art and Craftsmanship or *Kitsch?*

Critics of Fabergé's work often maintain that his functional objects should not be considered as art at all. Since the 19th century, the applied arts have generally been rated second to the fine arts, such as painting, architecture and sculpture, even if art historians did not clearly differentiate the two. It is correct to state that the applied arts are primarily concerned with the utilitarian aspect of an article—to which they add an aesthetic bonus, as it were, by giving it artistic form. In Fabergé's workshops, however, functional objects were designed in such a manner that the utilitarian aspect was merely an excuse for the production of a decorative work of art.

When considering the problem of art in connection with Fabergé, we should ask ourselves whether for an object to be a work of art the design and execution must be by the same hand and whether embellishment by a machine is necessarily excluded—a problem much discussed after the appearance of the jewellery industry at the turn of the century[14] and one that has often cropped up with regard to 'original' prints also. This question is relevant in so far as Carl Fabergé's activities were primarily of an organizational nature; of course, the business side of the firm and its artistic direction were closely associated, but we know of no article made personally by Carl Fabergé. However design ideas for individual articles regularly stemmed from Fabergé himself, but their execution—and that included finalizing the design—was the work of a staff of artist-craftsmen who, in the process of actually making the article, contributed their own ideas and skills. Moreover, before completion, the article passed through the hands of several groups of craftsmen: silversmiths, engravers, enamellers, all of whom worked on the same piece. Another notable feature of Fabergé's production process was its high degree of mechanization, particularly in the guilloché work, in which flat surfaces were engraved by machine. Yet it was Carl Fabergé's overall feeling for style, together with his knowledge of the different work processes involved, which ensured that each Fabergé article was consistent in design and workmanship. Since Fabergé also made it a principle never to produce two identical pieces, each and every item from the firm is an individual work of art of the highest craftsmanship.

Nevertheless, the fact remains that there can be a spontaneous reaction at Fabergé exhibitions to dismiss part of his work as *kitsch,* and in fact some of his output does lie on the verge of *kitsch;*[15] however the meaning of the term *kitsch* needs clarification. The German word *kitsch* has been in use since about 1870 to describe a fringe phenomenon of art aesthetics: a discrepancy between the presumed practical purpose of an object and the symbolic values upon which that object draws.[16] The classification '*kitsch*' need not exclude an object from having artistic value, since subjective criteria play such a predominant role in choosing this definition. An example may be seen in Plate 49, a match-holder shaped like a pig: the exaggerated realism of the figure can seem ridiculous to the beholder, who may then classify it as *kitsch.*

When people speak of *kitsch* in connection with Fabergé, they usually refer to his *objets de vitrine* (small objects for display), such as miniature replicas of furniture or hardstone figures realistically depicting ethnic types and made to be displayed as tiny works of art in a showcase. The impression created in both cases by the combination

49 Stone match-holder shaped as a pig and silver-mounted, 15.5 cm long, signed, made by the First Silver *Artel* (cooperative), 1908–17, for Fabergé. The matches can be lit on the roughened stone hide of the pig.

50 Silver table lighter shaped as a wolf's head protruding from a shawl.

49

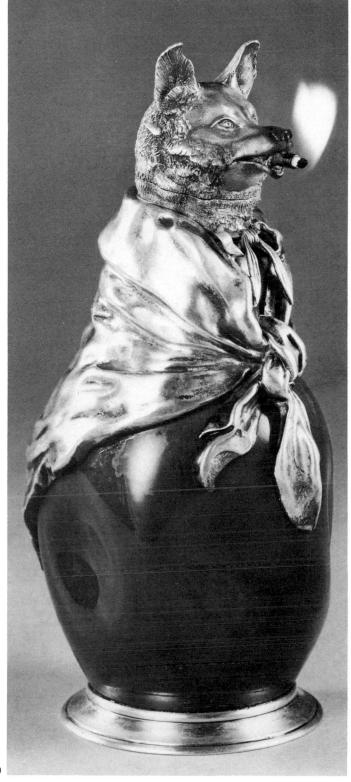

50

51

52

53

51 Miniature table of nephrite, gold-mounted; the red guilloché enamel sides have applied swags, 9 cm long, signed, workmaster Michael Perchin, 1899–1908 (no. 5853).

52 Gold bonbonnière shaped as a miniature table with a lapis-lazuli top; underneath it is enamelled in yellow, 8.8 cm high, signed, workmaster Michael Perchin.

53 Perpetual calender of silver gilt and yellow guilloché enamel on four paw feet; the calender has applied laurel swags and acanthus foliage, 12.5 cm high, workmaster Michael Perchin.

of the unexpected (perhaps even vulgar) and the precious in such unlovely objects as a dandelion seed-clock or a slimy frog in semiprecious stones is often disconcerting; yet Fabergé and his art objects were very close to the art of the renaissance and the baroque periods that valued and indeed collected such showpieces, whereas nowadays we are no longer accustomed to recognise the artistic value of such decorative objects that have no practical value and tend to dismiss them as *kitsch*.[17] This only provides further proof that the verdict '*kitsch*' is pronounced not on the basis of form and content alone, but is also coloured by the viewer's subjective relationship to the thing viewed, and the viewer in turn is always influenced by trends governing the artistic interpretation and fashion of his own period.

Although it is sometimes difficult to contradict those who use the term *kitsch* in connection with some of Fabergé's art, it may be said conclusively that the quality of workmanship of each individual Fabergé piece renders it 'satisfying' from an aesthetic point of view—reason enough for the majority of viewers to place these articles with the best of art.

Workshops and Craftsmen

St. Petersburg (1870–1918)

The firm of Gustav Fabergé occupied modest premises on the ground floor of a building in Bolshaya Morskaya Street. Following his son Carl's assumption of the management of the firm in 1870, the ever-increasing demand for Fabergé products and the consequent enlargement of the workshops necessitated a move to more spacious premises. Eventually, in 1900, Carl Fabergé purchased a handsome building in the same street, 24 Bolshaya Morskaya Street (Plate 7), that had enough floors to house all the principal workshops. On the ground floor, conveniently near the salerooms, was Carl Fabergé's own office; this was the hub of the organization. On the first floor were Fabergé's apartment and the workshop of the goldsmith August Hollming; the second floor housed the workshop of the head workmaster of the time (Kollin, Perchin or Wigström), the third that of the head jeweller, August Holmström, and the fourth another jewellery workshop under Alfred Thielemann. The gem-carving and silversmiths' workshops were the only ones not on the premises. The reason for this concentration of workshops in the one building lay in the structure of the Fabergé hierarchy, which culminated in the bearded figure of the benevolent, all-overseeing patriarch.

The production process began in Fabergé's office, for the inspiration for and artistic conception of a piece frequently stemmed from him, originally in collaboration with his brother Agathon (1862–1895). Getting the idea down on paper was the responsibility of the first draughtsman, the Swiss François Bierbaum, universally described as a brilliant graphic artist. He and the other designers (Plate 15) had the job of producing detailed drawings and planning the stages of manufacture. If necessary a conference would be held round the circular table in Fabergé's office. Then the head workmaster would receive the commission, and he would decide to which workshops—always under his own supervision—the different stages of manufacture should be assigned. Often the original design would be altered by the workmaster for technical reasons. In the case of major commissions, the piece would be submitted to Fabergé after each work process. The completed piece received his final approval in the form of a signature stamp bearing his name. Articles that did not come up to his standard of quality were either destroyed or sold without his signature.

Fabergé's chief associates in St. Petersburg were three head workmasters. Erik Kollin (1836–1901), a Scandinavian, had worked originally for August Holmström, who had his own workshop. From 1870 to 1886 Kollin managed all the Fabergé workshops. It was he who was responsible for the copies made of the Scythian gold treasures found at Kertch in the Crimea, for which the firm received the Nuremberg gold medal in 1885. Kollin specialized in gold and filigree work and had an archaizing style comparable with that of the 19th-century Italian goldsmiths Giuliano and Castellani (Plate 26). Probably the first imperial Easter Eggs, and certainly that of 1884, were made by him. His mark is E. K. (see p. 153).

Kollin's successor was Michael Perchin (1860–1903), a man of Russian peasant stock who took over the management of the workshops in 1886. His style has much

54 Gold frame with a laurel-leaf border and a cabochon moonstone as a finial; there are applied swags in varicoloured gold and cabochon rubies on the gold foot, 8 cm high, signed, workmaster Victor Aarne, 1899–1908 (no. 3346). Miniature photographs can be displayed in both the front and back of this frame.

55 Miniature frame of gold and white enamel; the backing is made of mother-of-pearl, 14.8 cm high, signed, workmaster Henrik Wigström.

56 Nephrite tankard with fluted gold cover, engraved with the coat-of-arms of a Russian Grand Duke, 16 cm high, signed, workmaster Michael Perchin, English import marks.

57 Nephrite vase in the Mogul style, decorated with arabesques in gold, with emerald, sapphire, ruby, cabochons and with diamonds, 12.5 cm high, signed, workmaster Michael Perchin, 1899–1908.

58 Triangular table clock of gold and concentric mauve guilloché enamel, set with three oval plaques of moss agate, 13 cm high, signed, workmaster Michael Perchin.
Trefoil-shaped triple photograph frame of enamelled gold; the transparent and opalescent salmon-coloured enamel is laid over a sunburst and flame guilloché pattern, 10 cm high, signed, workmaster Michael Perchin. (Formerly Princess Henry of Prussia, sister of the last tsarina, Alexandra Feodorovna.)
Octagonal frame of silver-gilt and honey-coloured guilloché enamel, 8.5 cm high, signed with initials and imperial warrant mark, c. 1880. This is one of the rare examples of guilloché enamel from the Moscow workshops.

54

55

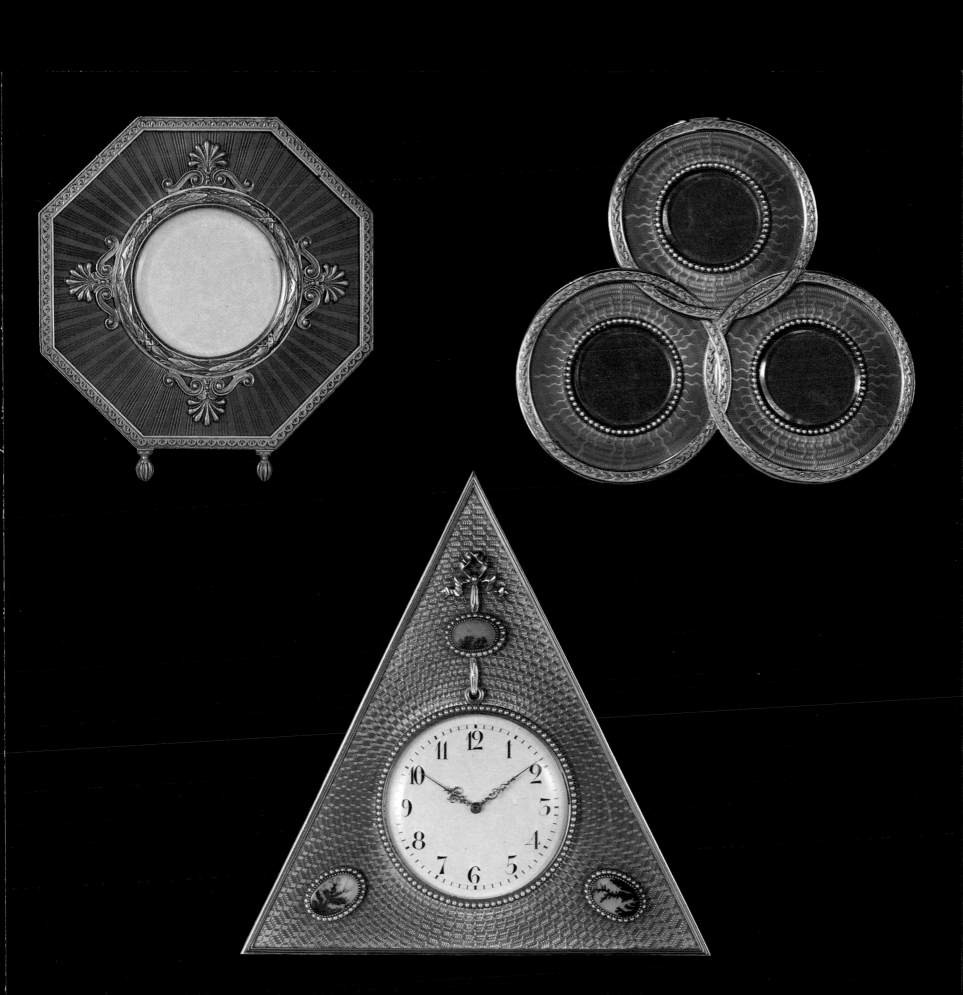

of baroque and rococo in it; most objects containing rocaille elements (Plate 47) can confidently be attributed to his hand. Since it was during Perchin's time as head workmaster that the firm began to enjoy its first successes, his name is often—and with some justification—identified with the House of Fabergé as a whole (see pp. 153–4).

From Perchin's death in 1903 to the break-up of the firm in 1918, the post of head workmaster was occupied by his former chief assistant, Henrik Wigström (1862–1930?). The fact that many more articles bear the mark H.W. (see p. 154) than Perchin's mark is due to the big increase in the size of the firm after 1900. The flowers and the hardstones were assembled in his workshop. Technically perfect, his pieces usually feature elements of Louis XVI and Empire styles (e.g. Plate 33). Extensive use of acanthus and laurel-leaf bands in his late period often led to a somewhat stereotyped effect.

The other workmasters all came under the head workmaster of the time. August Wilhelm Holmström (1829–1903), the senior member of the firm, had been with the Fabergé's since Gustav's day. He headed the jewellery workshop, and the finest pieces of jewellery bear his mark AH (see p. 153), as does the 1892 Easter Egg (Cat. Plate 9) made for the tsar's wife. Anders Nevalainen (1858-) worked under Holmström; he was apprenticed in 1876 and became a workmaster in 1885. His mark— A.N. (see p. 153)—is also found on articles from the Moscow workshops.

Johan Viktor Aarne (1863-) joined Fabergé in 1891. His mark is B.A. (see p. 153), and it appears on some outstanding articles in gold and enamel. He was succeeded by Karl Gustav Hjalmar Armfeld, whose Я A. mark (see p. 153) figures on later works. August Hollming (1854–1915), apprenticed in 1876 and a workmaster from 1880 onwards, specialized in gold and enamel. Many enamelled brooches and other pieces of jewellery bear his mark, A*H, which is often confused with that of Holmström (see p. 153). Fedor Afanassiev was well-known for his small *objets de fantaisie*, Gabriel Niukkanen for his gold cigarette cases, Vladimir Soloviev for enamelled silver. The two head enamellers of the firm, Alexander Petrov and Vassili Boitzov, did not have marks of their own.

Away from the main building, the silversmith Julius Rappoport (1864–1916), who began working for Fabergé in 1883, had his workshop on the Ekaterininsky Canal. His mark—I.P. (see p. 154)—can also be found on many Moscow pieces; his preference was for the Louis XVI style. An associate of his, Stephan Wäkevä, marked his work. S.W. (see p. 154). Karl Woerffel's hardstone workshop, which Fabergé took over at an early stage, was on the Obvodny Canal, and under him, working in total anonymity, the three artists Kremlev, Derbyshev, and Svetchnikov turned out animal figures and flowers.

In addition to these workmasters Fabergé's St. Petersburg staff included many designers, miniaturists—including the court painter Vassili Zuiev (Plate 121)—and modellers, together of course with a large number of ordinary craftsmen. Something like twenty craftsmen were employed just to make the maple-wood cases for the individual pieces (Plate 167).

As far as the workmasters were concerned, working conditions in the House of Fabergé were ideal. They had no investments of their own to make in the expensive materials of their trade, because all the necessary gems and metals were provided for them, and the fact that the workshops were all situated so close together made possible

59 *(left row):* Parasol handle of gold and yellow guilloché enamel with a seed-pearl border, 4.5 cm high, signed, workmaster Michael Perchin. Paperclip of silver and blue guilloché enamel with a gold mount, 4.9 cm high, signed, workmaster Fedor Afanassiev, 1908–17. Stamp box of silver-gilt and violet guilloché enamel with an original stamp under glass, 4 cm long, workmaster Henrik Wigström.
(centre): Clock of mauve guilloché enamel, mounted in silver-gilt on a wooden pedestal, 16.9 cm high, signed, workmaster Victor Aarne, before 1899.
(right row): Parasol handle in gold and primrose-yellow enamel similar to the one on the left but with a different guilloché pattern, 5 cm high, workmaster Michael Perchin, before 1899. Vodka cup of silver-gilt and red guilloché enamel with green enamel borders, 4.2 cm high, signed, rare mark of workmaster Wilhelm Reimers, 1899–1908. Miniature table clock of silver-gilt and blue enamel, 5 cm high, signed, workmaster Henrik Wigström, 1908–17.

a continuous exchange of ideas among the artist-craftsmen concerned. However for the ordinary craftsmen working at Fabergé's, overtime and even Sunday work were the rule (Plates 9–12).

The products of Fabergé's St. Petersburg workshops are quite different from those of his other branches. They have an elegance, a refinement, and a perfection of workmanship all their own. From St. Petersburg came only the transparent guilloché enamel, never the heavier cloisonné type (see Materials and Techniques). Fabergé's international court style achieved full expression only in St. Petersburg, where his clients came mainly from the western-influenced aristocracy.

Moscow (1887–1918)

The Moscow clientèle, on the other hand, belonged to a *nouveau riche* class of the bourgeoisie with strong traditional ties, and the workshops there were geared mainly to producing silverware and cloisonné enamel. This type of work, done in a pan-Slavic (based on the medieval period in Russia) as well as a certain amount of art-nouveau pieces characterizes the output of Fabergé's Moscow branch. It was precisely this national traditionalism—which the St. Petersburgers tended to disparage as 'merchant's style'—that kept the clientèle limited to the Moscow region. It is noticeable that in 1902 and 1914 the well-known German travel guide *Baedeker* made no special mention of the branch for the benefit of foreign visitors.

The hierarchical structure was very different from that existing at St. Petersburg. A branch manager took the place of Fabergé himself—originally the English brothers Allan, Arthur, and Charles Bowe as partners, then from 1906 Otto Jarke, followed by Andrea Marchetti and finally by Alexander Fabergé. Altogether a hundred craftsmen were employed by the Moscow branch. Most of the designers and workshop managers were of Russian origin. Michael Tcherpunov headed the large silversmith's workshop, Oskar Pihl the jewellery workshop (see p. 154), and Gustav Jahr the one producing *objets de vitrine* (small objects for display). Fedor Rückert, the only cloisonné-enamel workmaster, had his own independent workshop (see p. 154); he did not work exclusively for Fabergé.

Odessa (1890–1918) and Kiev (1905–1910)

These less important branches had their own branch managers, workmasters, and designers. In Odessa, Vladimir Nikolaev headed a workshop with twenty-five employees engaged in making small pieces of jewellery. The Kiev branch was closed after only five years in order to concentrate the entire south-Russian market at Odessa.

London (1903–1915)

The London branch was started in 1903, initially as a contact office in Berners Hotel. Arthur Bowe travelled to London with a selection of articles from the Moscow workshop. Bowe, a partner in the firm, ran the London office almost as an off-shoot of the Moscow branch, but when he left the firm (in 1906) Carl Fabergé opened a shop in London that was in direct touch with the St. Petersburg headquarters. It was managed by his son Nicholas in collaboration with Henry C. Bainbridge, and its last address was 173 New Bond Street. It was Fabergé's only foreign branch, and it was where the English royal family and their friends did their buying (Plates 158 and 159). It also provided a base for international contacts, and towards the end it was the main source of commissions from western Europe and America.

There was a small workshop in London in addition to the salerooms, but this was not so much for manufacturing complete articles as for assembling and altering or repairing pieces imported from Russia and for engraving dedications. Nevertheless, the London workshop was so organized that a designer and two modellers could work there, producing ideas that were then usually executed in St. Petersburg.

The necessity of importing objects from Russia led to a lawsuit against Fabergé instituted by the Goldsmiths Company: the English Customs Act of 1842 stipulated that all wares in precious metals must necessarily be hallmarked upon importation. Since the major part of Fabergé's importations were in guilloché enamel, hallmarking was rendered impossible or tremendously difficult (see Materials and Techniques). Thus after the adverse judgement of the courts it became necessary for Fabergé to dispatch all objects to London in half-finished state for marking, before the enamel coat was applied[18].

Due to the First World War, Fabergé's foreign clientèle travelled less freely than before, and the acquisition of such luxury articles as Fabergé produced could no longer be considered a primary necessity while all of Europe was involved in bloody battles. By imperial decree all the foreign capital of Russian nationals had to be repatriated, whereupon Fabergé closed his London branch in November, 1915. The French jewellers Lacloche Frères acquired the business and the stock, totalling approximately one hundred pieces. The linings of Fabergé's maple-wood cases were stamped with Lacloche's trademark. Apparently these objects could only be disposed of with difficulty in the early 1920s, since the magic of Fabergé's name and of royal patronage was no longer there. Nevertheless on an unofficial basis sales continued right through until January, 1917, as shown by the London sales ledgers in the Fabergé family's archives: on 20 December 1916, the following entry was made: 'H. M. Queen Alexandra: Box, silver, enamel painting of Czar's falconers £ 21 ($96)'.

The same source gives the turnover of the London branch between 14 July 1912 and 13 July 1913 as totalling £ 16 401 for 713 objects. This corresponds to the average annual turnover of the London office.

In spite of the fact that his objects were in high demand in Paris, Fabergé opened no office in the French capital. Catering for his French clientèle, Nicholas Fabergé undertook regular trips to Paris, mostly during December of each year, for in the spring, French and Russian aristocracy flocked to the Côte d'Azur. For this reason Nicholas travelled to Cannes, Nice and Monte Carlo every year in order to meet this portion of his clientèle and offer them Fabergé's latest productions, especially the much sought-after miniature Easter eggs (Plate 124). Business with the Roman nobility also attracted Nicholas Fabergé: several successful trips to the Italian capital are confirmed by the London sales ledgers.

Materials and Techniques

Gold, Silver, and Platinum

The gold used by Fabergé was the usual sort of goldsmith's alloy made by mixing pure gold (which is relatively soft) with other metals to produce the right degree of hardness both for working purposes and for withstanding wear and tear in the finished article. The House of Fabergé worked mainly with the 14-carat gold most widely in use in Russia; 18-carat gold is found only in important pieces, which are also distinguished by particularly careful workmanship and by choice gemstones.

The technical requirement of mixing gold with other metals has always inspired goldsmiths to make a virtue of necessity by aiming at particular colour effects. It is well known that the addition of silver can give the natural yellow of pure gold a greenish tinge; copper can be added to produce red gold and nickel or palladium to produce white gold. These basic colours were used particularly by French goldsmiths in the latter half of the 18th century, who talked about *or en quatre couleurs* ('four-colour gold'). In addition to this traditional palette, Fabergé set about mixing even rarer shades—blue, orange, and grey—by experimenting with different alloys. Fabergé's work with these alloys in fact owed a great deal to the art of the 18th-century French goldsmiths. His debt to 18th-century art is particularly apparent in the chasing of flower garlands in three or four shades of gold, with individual flowers, each a different colour, modelled in relief against a wreath of green-gold leaves (Plate 61). Garlands of this kind are generally used to break up areas of smooth enamel, to which they are attached with pins. Another exemplary aspect of Fabergé's work was his use of decorative motifs—rosettes, Empire palmettes, foliage friezes—in mat gold on areas of polished gold, giving the latter a three-dimensional quality (Plate 58). Fabergé also discovered new and effective ways of using gold. One idea that was Fabergé's own was to juxtapose sizeable areas of gold in a variety of shades. This is well illustrated by those cigarette cases (Plate 38) with ribbed or smooth surfaces and bands of red and yellow gold, or flutes in different shades of gold, radiating from a single point. It is the cigarette cases and the various other types of box that most strikingly demonstrate the quality of workmanship and the sheer virtuosity of Fabergé's goldsmiths. The joints in the lids are so neat and the lids fit so snugly as to make catches superfluous: the boxes stay shut by themselves. The hinges, too, show the same sort of precision; they are fitted inside the box or case so that they are barely visible from outside and interrupt the smoothness of the gold surface only minimally (Plate 165).

Silver was used in Russia in three grades of purity, although Fabergé most often used the two higher grades, bearing the *zolotnik* marks 88 and 91 (96 *zolotniks* is pure silver, see Hallmarks). It was above all the Moscow workshops that specialized in the manufacture of all-silver wares such as table silver, candlesticks, and centrepieces. They employed a novel type of ornamental technique that consisted in artificially blackening pieces of silver by oxidization to make them stand out against a lighter silver background. The technique was much used on articles in the Romanov Tercentenary style. Fabergé produced very little work using niello decoration, which

60 Four types of bell push in various materials and techniques: *(left to right):* Silver-gilt bell push with white guilloché enamel, 5.3 cm wide, signed, workmaster Victor Aarne. Bowenite bell push mounted in silver-gilt, 4.8 cm high, signed, workmaster Victor Aarne, 1899–1908. Chalcedony bell push, enamelled gold mount, 5.9 cm long, signed, workmaster Michael Perchin. Gold bell push with white guilloché enamel and a cabochon sapphire push-piece, 4.6 cm wide, signed, workmaster Victor Aarne.

61 A particularly well-made nephrite frame, gold-mounted and enamelled, 12.5 cm high, workmaster Michael Perchin. The floral swags give a fine example of the use of four-colour gold in Fabergé's workshops.

62 Gold cigarette case with tapering flutes in two-colour gold and a cabochon sapphire push-piece, 8.4 cm long, workmaster August Holmström.
Cigarette case of engine-turned gold with chased foliage borders in varicoloured gold, 8.5 cm long, signed, workmaster Henrik Wigström, English import marks.

63 Cigarette case of reeded gold with curved oval section and a cabochon sapphire thumbpiece, 8.5 cm long, signed.
Two-colour gold cigarette case, engine-turned, with a rose-diamond thumbpiece, 8 cm long, signed, workmaster Henrik Wigström; made for the English market.

64 Silver ashtray on four ball feet, set with a 1775 silver rouble, 8 cm wide, signed, workmaster Victor Aarne 1899–1908 (no. 1670). Silver beaker chased with scrolls, 7.5 cm high, imperial warrant mark, Moscow, before 1899.

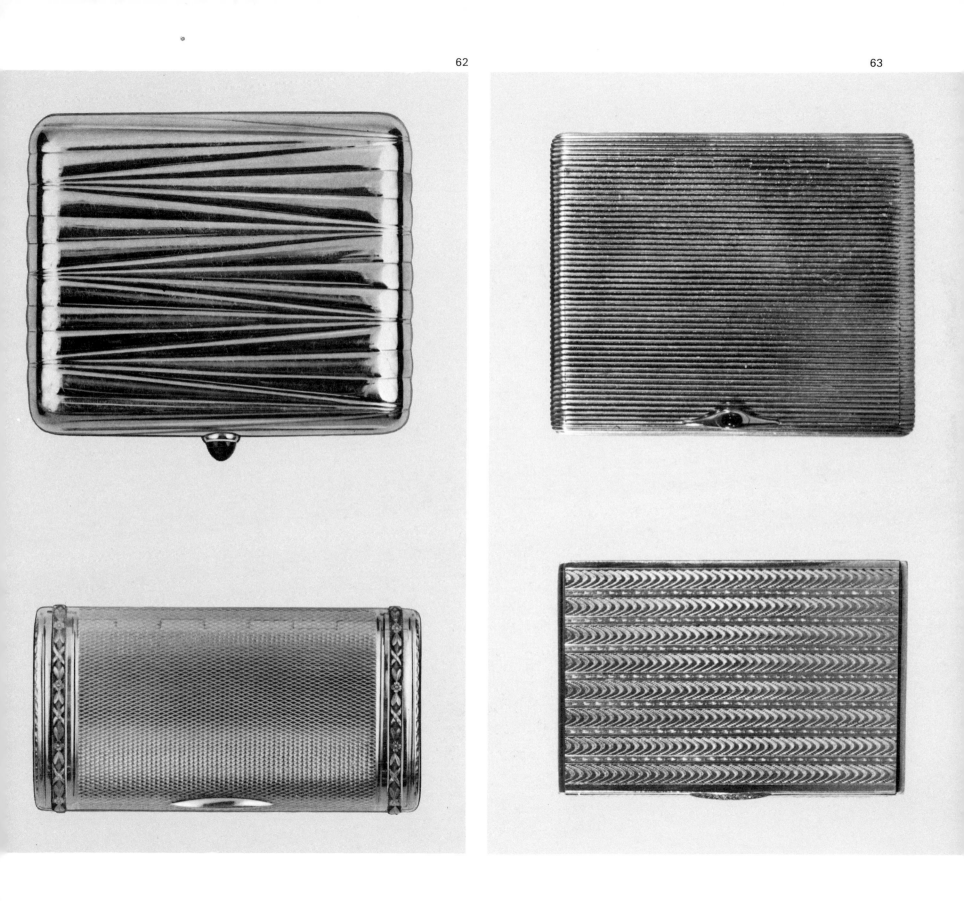

66

67

69

68

70

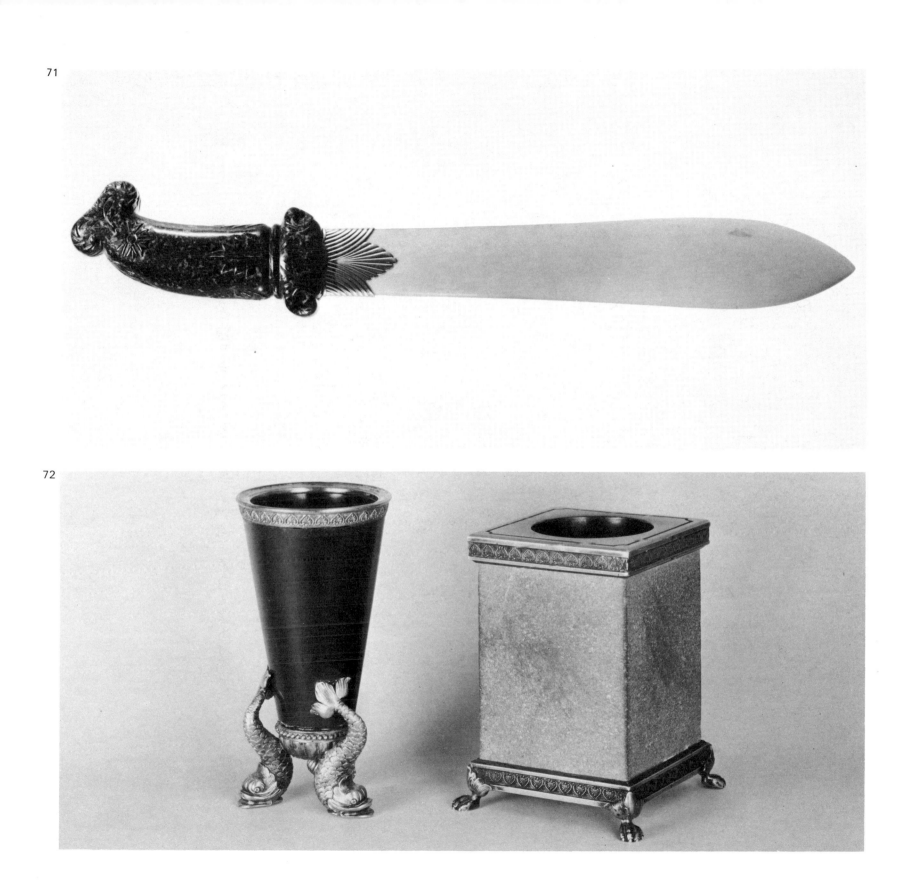

71

72

65 Two silver vodka cups shaped as elephants with garnet eyes; the animals are portrayed in typical positions: *(left)* 4 cm high, workmaster Henrik Wigström, 1899–1908 (no. 11692); *(right)* 4 cm high, workmaster Henrik Wigström, 1908–1917; *(centre)* Conical silver beaker, 6.5 cm high, imperial warrant mark, Moscow, 1908–17.

66 Part of a silver coffee set in the rococo style; the coffee-pot is 13.5 cm high, imperial warrant mark, Moscow, 1895.

67 Silver tea and coffee set with ivory handles; the coffee-pot is 18.2 cm high, imperial warrant mark, workmaster I. W., St. Petersburg, 1899–1908 (no. 10878).

68 Earthenware jug with silver-gilt cover, inspired by a 17th-century English object, 17.5 cm high, signed, workmaster Julius Rappoport, before 1899.

69 Oval faience vase, silver-mounted, 13.5 cm long, workmaster K. B. (in the original Fabergé case).

70 Silver-mounted faience bowl, 8 cm across, workmaster Anders Nevalainen.

71 Ivory paperknife mounted in gold with a lapis-lazuli handle, 37 cm long, workmaster Henrik Wigström, 1899–1908. The handle, probably of Persian origin, was mounted by Fabergé at the request of Othmar Neuscheller.

72 Grey stone inkwell, silver-mounted, 7 cm high, imperial warrant mark, workmaster Julius Rappoport, St. Petersburg, before 1899.
Brown glass vase, mounted in silver-gilt, 8 cm high, signed, workmaster Michael Perchin, St. Petersburg, before 1899.

73 Silver-mounted occasional table of palisander with a nephrite top, in the Louis XVI style, 66 cm high, 63.5 cm across, signed, by the First Silver *Artel*. From Fabergé's apartment in the Bolshaya Morskaya Street, where it was discovered in 1918 after he emigrated.

involved filling engraved lines in a silver surface with a black lead alloy. Though the technique had been popular in Russia for centuries, Fabergé probably found that it left him too little artistic freedom. The Moscow workshops were also responsible for those interesting cases in *samorodok* (nugget-like) silver, having surfaces resembling a raw nugget of metal (Plate 144, bottom, an example from a competitor). This effect was achieved by heating the metal to just below its melting-point and then cooling it abruptly; the same technique was used in gold. Moscow also turned out a series of silver animal figures large in size, many of them mounted on stone bases (Plate 103).

While Moscow made extensive use of silver for its own sake, producing articles that often have a heavy, even clumsy look about them, in St. Petersburg the metal was used in an entirely different way. Here the emphasis was on treating silver surfaces with the widest variety of technical and artistic means. Silver served as the basis for guilloché enamelled surfaces or was heavily gilded. In St. Petersburg even the Louis XVI-style flower garlands were done in four-colour gilding (Plate 24, right).

Fabergé used platinum in special cases—one of them is the Alexander III Equestrian Egg of 1910 (Plate 125), though chains were often made in this metal. This reserve in the use of platinum is due to the fact that around 1900 it was considered far less valuable than gold[19]. As in most countries, a Russian hallmark for platinum did not exist.

Base Metals, Unconventional Materials and Prefabricated Parts

A number of Fabergé articles are remarkable for the fact that they use materials not normally employed by goldsmiths. These include not only base metals but also wood, glass, and porcelain, usually in gold, silver, or enamel settings. The articles in question typify Fabergé's attitude to materials in general: to him it was not the commercial value of a piece of work that counted so much as the decorative value invested in it by the workmanship of his craftsmen.

One of Fabergé's favorite base metals was blued steel, which is extremely effective when used in conjunction with gold. As well as making cigarette cases with it, Fabergé used the gleaming effect of blued steel in imperial Easter Eggs: the Romanov Tercentenary Egg of 1913 (Plate 121)—made, as usual, of gold with enamelling—contained a surprise in the shape of a blued-steel globe on which the farflung borders of the Russian empire were picked out in gilt. The Easter Egg that Tsar Nicholas II gave the Tsarina in 1916 is largely made of steel (Cat. Plate 56).

During the First World War many articles were made of iron or copper, owing to shortages of materials and undoubtedly also to a certain obligatory restraint. Often these bore the inscription '1914 War' in addition to the name of Fabergé.

Ornamental considerations dictated Fabergé's use of polished wood. His favourites were Karelian birch, elder, rosewood, and mahogany. Particularly attractive are the picture frames that use burr wood in conjunction with guilloché enamelling, which appears to imitate the structure of the wood. Apart from frames, cases, bell pushes, and so on, Fabergé also made large pieces of wooden furniture—mostly occasional tables and tables—with silver mounts, nor must we forget the maple-wood cases that were specially made for each Fabergé article and exhibit a standard of workmanship that makes them entirely worthy of their contents.

In addition to the materials mentioned above, which Fabergé used in his own workshops, we also find articles in porcelain, faience, or glass to which Fabergé contributed no more than the setting. Most of the porcelain, which was less commonly used than earthenware came from the Imperial Porcelain Factory, St. Petersburg; earthenware came from the Stroganoff school, Moscow, from Rörstrand, Sweden, or from English sources.

As for glass, around 1900 in particular, Fabergé made settings for a number of articles by Gallé and Tiffany[20].

Most of Fabergé's watch-movements were commissioned from the Swiss watch-makers Paul Buhré or Henri Moser. It should be noted that Fabergé's dials with Arabic numerals and elegant watch-hands nearly all follow a set type and are often of a standard 4.5-centimetre diameter.

Enamel

Fabergé's superb enamelling technique is regarded as one of his main contributions to art at the end of the last century[21]. His thorough knowledge of 18th-century goldsmith's work and in particular of the enamelling on Louis XV and Louis XVI snuffboxes lay at the basis of all his work in this medium. It was this period too that provided the stimulus for his ventures in the enamelling of larger surfaces, an extremely intricate technique known as *en plein* (all-over) enamel.

The enamellers employed in the head workmaster's workshop were Alexander Petrov, later joined by his son Nicholas, and Vassili Boitzov, together with a staff of craftsmen. Working in total anonymity—they had no signature rights—these men produced the miracles of enamelling for which Fabergé became famous.

Enamelling involves heating a compound of glass and metal oxides until it begins to run and then applying it to a metal surface that an engraver has patterned in advance. The commonest types of such guilloché work on enamelled articles by Fabergé are wave (or moiré) designs, but his engravers were continually experimenting with new combinations of engraved lines, producing some startling effects (Plate 74). Fabergé was also permanently in search of new enamel colours, and 144 different basic shades have been catalogued[22]. The large number of possible combinations of enamel colours and guilloché patterns goes a long way towards explaining the versatility for which Fabergé was renowned.

Clear enamel melts at about 600°C (1112°F), opaque enamel at 300°C (572°F). It was nearly always applied to silver, because for certain enamel colours—green, for example—this gave the best results; more rarely, gold was used. In order to strengthen the enamel coating, the article was heated several times in the kiln and further coats of enamel applied. This very tricky process called for the greatest precision, particularly when the piece being enamelled was not flat but spherical or egg-shaped.

The special brilliance of Fabergé's enamel was often achieved by applying a coat of platinum over the engine-turned silver surface.

74 A selection of examples of Fabergé's guilloché work, including the moiré, wave and sunburst patterns.

75 Gold case for ball programmes; pink translucent enamel over a sunburst guilloché pattern, painted with dendritic markings, 9 cm long, signed.
Gold-mounted card case of silver in green translucent enamel over an unusual laurel-leaf pattern, 8.5 cm long, workmaster Henrik Wigström.

76 Parasol handle of gold and green guilloché enamel, surmounted by a nephrite frog with rose-diamonds for eyes, 12 cm high, workmaster Henrik Wigström.
Tcharka (vodka cup) of silver and reddish brown guilloché enamel; the handle is made from a 1751 rouble, 6 cm across, workmaster Anders Nevalainen.
Oblong thermometer of silver-gilt and pink guilloché enamel, 12 cm high, workmaster Victor Aarne.

77 Three enamelled frames for miniatures. Gold frame with yellow guilloché enamel, 8.1 cm high, signed, workmaster Michael Perchin, before 1899. Frame of gold and pink guilloché enamel with applied varicoloured floral swags, 8.8 cm high, workmaster Hjalmar Armfelt, 1899–1908 (nos. 14330 and 26428). Frame of silver-gilt with yellow sunburst guilloché enamel and applied laurel swags, 9.4 cm high, signed, workmaster Michael Perchin, 1899–1908.

78 Three miniature photograph frames of gold with various guilloché patterns: *(left to right)* 6.5 cm high, workmaster Hjalmar Armfelt; 7.3 cm high, workmaster Hjalmar Armfelt; 7 cm high, workmaster Michael Perchin. All three have ivory backings.

77▲ ▼78

79 Clock of gold and green guilloché enamel with applied swags in two-colour gold, 10.5 across, signed, workmaster Henrik Wigström, 1899–1908 (no. 11214).

80 Clock of gold and pink guilloché enamel with applied wreathes in varicoloured gold, 9.5 cm across, signed, workmaster Michael Perchin, before 1899.

81 Gold cigarette case with blue translucent enamel over a moiré guilloché pattern, inset on both sides with a band of rose-cut diamonds forming a serpent, 9.7 cm long, signed K. Fabergé in Cyrillic characters. Given to King Edward VII of England by Mrs. George Keppel. (Collection of Her Majesty the Queen).

82 Cigarette case of gold and pale blue guilloché enamel, complete with a tinder cord and a miniature Easter-egg pendant of enamelled gold on a gold chain, 10.3 cm long, signed, workmaster Michael Perchin.
Gold bonbonnière with white guilloché enamel; the lid is set with a large scarab made of turquoise from the Ural Mountains, 7.8 cm long, signed.

83 Silver bell push, gold-mounted, with pale violet enamel and a push-piece consisting of a cabochon moonstone, 6.8 cm high, workmaster Hjalmar Armfelt.
Beaker of silver-gilt and green guilloché enamel, shaped as a *bratina* (punch bowl) and set with half-rouble pieces of Elizabeth I and Catherine II. The lip is chased with foliage and set with rubies, 6 cm high, workmaster Anders Nevalainen.

84 Gold cigarette case with ochre-coloured enamel over a sunburst guilloché pattern, 8.5 cm long, signed, workmaster Michael Perchin, 1899–1908.
Silver-gilt cigarette case with scarlet enamel over an excentric sunburst guilloché pattern; there is an applied decoration of a double-headed eagle made of gold and set with diamonds, 15 cm long, signed, workmaster Michael Perchin, 1899–1908.

85 *(top row)* Pair of rectangular gold cuff-links, enamelled and set with four sapphires of different colours, workmaster August Hollming, 1899–1908. Pair of circular gold cuff-links, enamelled and set with cabochon rubies, signed, workmaster Henrik Wigström, before 1899.
(second row) Heart-shaped pendant of enamelled gold, set with sapphires and diamonds, before 1899. Rare gold pendant watch set with gems and enamelled, suspended from a bar brooch that is set with rectangular-cut sapphires and rose-diamonds, 5.5 cm high. (The brooch is by workmaster August Thielemann, 1908–17; the watch by Moser & Co.; no. AT 17915). Enamelled gold pendant for a photograph, 3 cm across, signed with initials, workmaster August Hollming.
(third row) Circular moonstone brooch, 2.4 cm brooch, enamelled, set with a Mecca stone cabochon, 2.8 cm across, unmarked (no. 85939).
(bottom) Enamelled gold lorgnette, 13.5 cm long, workmaster Michael Perchin.

86 Cigarette case of silver-gilt and scarlet guilloché enamel over a wave pattern, engine-turned, 8.5 cm long, workmaster August Hollming.

Cigarette case of gold and green guilloché enamel over a sunburst pattern, engine-turned; the lines are made of rose-diamonds, 8.8 cm long, workmaster August Hollming.

87 Gold table clock in grey enamel over a wave and flame guilloché pattern; the clock face is surrounded by pearls, 12 cm high, signed, workmaster Henrik Wigström, 1899–1908 (Wartski's, London).

88 Star-shaped clock of gold, nephrite and opalescent guilloché enamel, painted with dendritic motifs, 13.2 cm high, workmaster Michael Perchin. (Formerly probably from the imperial yacht Polar Star).

89–90 Sedan-chair of gold with pink enamel panels over sunburst guilloché patterns that are gilded and painted with emblems of Art, Love and Gardening. The interior is fitted in mother-of-pearl, 9.1 cm high, signed, workmaster Michael Perchin, 1899–1908 (no. 2707). All types of Fabergé's enamelling techniques are represented in this fine piece.

91 *Bratina* (punch bowl) of silver-gilt and cloisonné enamel, depicting a double-headed eagle, 24 cm high, imperial warrant mark, Moscow, 1899–1908. Presented by Nicholas II to the French admiral Germinet in May, 1902. This is a typical example of the Moscow branch's production; the shape and style are borrowed from Russian models of the 17th century, while the decoration—in Fedor Rückert's pastel-coloured palette—is derived from art nouveau.

The ultimate refinement in enamelling technique consists in applying successive coats of enamel in slight gradations of colour, which is how the opalescent effect known as 'oyster enamel' was achieved (Plate 148). Here the enameller laid down a semi-transparent coat in a warm orange colour and covered it with further coats of clear white enamel; when the article is moved in the light it shimmers with different colours, the effect being enhanced by the guilloché pattern underneath. Often the enameller would paint flowers and trees on the penultimate coat (Plate 88). A few pieces feature a flat enamel painting: a portrait, perhaps, or an allegory of the kind found on 18th-century snuffboxes (Plate 154).

Fabergé's enamel work is noted for its velvety smoothness, a quality achieved only by hours of dedicated polishing with a wooden wheel and wash-leather (chammy). It is a lengthy process, for which present-day craftsmen can hardly afford the time.

Contrasting with the elegance of flat-surface enamelling is the rather clumsier technique known a cloisonné enamelling which had a long tradition in Russia. In this, wires are welded on to the silver surface in such a way as to separate and contain small areas or cells (cloisons in French) of enamel in different colours arranged in an arabesque pattern. The technique had been used by many silversmiths in the second half of the 19th century, but Fabergé's mastercraftsman for cloisonné enamel, Fedor Rückert, took it further. In his work the welded wires do more than just outline the enamel cells; they form patterns of their own, often in the shape of spirals or pellets. Moreover Rückert almost invariably finished his pieces with a coating of enamel all over so that they give the impression of an evenly enamelled surface; the colours are limited in the main to pastel shades. Another remarkable feature of his work is that the wires were very often gilded after the enamelling process had been completed, making the final effect even more colourful (Plate 91).

Champlevé enamelling—the technique, also common in Russia, of filling engraved patterns with enamel—was practised by Fabergé only in the Renaissance style.

Hardstones

The Russian hardstone-carving trade, centred on Ekaterinenburg, enjoyed a period of great brilliance during the 19th century, as did those of Germany and Italy. Not long after 1884 Fabergé, always on the lookout for new modes of expression, established links with Karl Woerffel's workshop on the Obvodny Canal in St. Petersburg; later that workshop became part of the firm. From 1900 onwards, probably under the management of the German Alexander Meier, this workshop played an increasingly important role. This was where the gem-carvers Kremlev, Derbyshev, and Svetchnikov produced their flowers, animals, and human figures. Fabergé also commissioned hardstone objects (mostly in nephrite) from the Imperial Harstone Workshops in the town of Peterhof. This is proved by the marks on the maple-wood cases for the items in question. The man responsible for selecting the gems and hardstones was Fabergé's second son, Agathon, who was the firm's expert on precious and semiprecious stones. It was this Agathon who, shortly after 1918, was commissioned by the Soviet government to catalogue the Russian crown jewels[23].

92 A seal made of obsidian on a rock-crystal base simulating ice; the seal is 12 cm long. Formerly the collection of Miss Yznaga, London, sister of the Duchess of Manchester, one of Fabergé's Edwardian patrons, who owned a large Fabergé collection during the 1930 s.

93 Examples of animals in Fabergé's 'geometric' style: kingfishers and sparrows made of various hardstones. The kingfisher on the left is made of nephrite with gold feet, 4.8 cm high, workmaster Henrik Wigström. (Collection of H. M. the Queen, Sandringham).

94 Nephrite bonbonnière, gold-mounted and shaped as a miniature piano, 7 cm long, signed in an enamel plaque, workmaster Michael Perchin. (Collection of H. M. the Queen, Sandringham).

95 A capstan-shaped inkwell made of nephrite and gold-mounted, 10.5 cm high, workmaster Michael Perchin.

96 Silver occasional table with a nephrite top, in the Empire style, 95 cm high, 57 cm across, signed, workmaster Hjalmar Armfelt.

97 Two small gold-mounted frames of nephrite with applied swags of varicoloured gold and cabochon rubies: (left) 6.5 cm high, signed, workmaster Victor Aarne, 1899–1908 (no.7930); (right) 8.5 cm high, signed, workmaster Hjalmar Armfelt, 1899–1908 (no.13102). Both frames have a mother-of-pearl backing instead of the more usual ivory plaques.

98 Oval box of nephrite, gold-mounted; the cover is set with a plaque of dendritic moss agate, 8.3 cm long, signed, workmaster Henrik Wigström, 1908–17 (no.25479).

99 Octagonal box made of nephrite and gold-mounted; the lid is set with a moss-agate plaque, 8.5 cm long, signed, workmaster Henrik Wigström, 1908–17 (no.21438).

107

108

100 Grey chalcedony elephant seated on its hind quarters, 4.7 cm high.

101 Nephrite bison with rose-diamond eyes, 4.9 cm long.

102 Three elephants: *(left to right)* made of rock crystal with an enamelled gold howdah, 2.5 cm high; a steel automaton, 5 cm high; made of sardonyx, 2.5 cm high. (Collection of H. M. the Queen, Sandringham).

103 A silver serpent on a block of turquoise, 19.5 cm high, workmaster Victor Aarne. (Formerly Robert Strauss Collection, Stonehurst).

104 Three animal carvings of agate: *(left to right)* a duckling with gold feet and rose-diamond eyes, 4.2 cm high; a capercailzie with gold feet and rose-diamond eyes, 7 cm high; a hare with emerald eyes, 6 cm high. (Formerly collection of Miss Yznaga, London).

105 Agate ostrich with rose-diamond eyes and chased gold legs, 8.4 cm high. (Collection of Her Majesty the Queen).

106 Agate kiwi with rose-diamond eyes and chased gold legs and beak, 5.1 cm high, gold mark 72, workmaster Henrik Wigström. (Collection of Her Majesty the Queen).

107 Dormouse of blue-grey-brown agate with cabochon sapphire eyes, nibbling on gold straws, 6.5 cm high. Described in the sales ledger of Fabergé's London branch (see Pl. 158): 'Queen Alexandra, Dormouse, agate, gold straws, 2 cab, sapphs: no. 22031, £33/–/ ($160).' (Collection of Her Majesty the Queen).

108 Koala-bear made of honey-coloured agate with emerald eyes, climbing on a silver branch; the koala is 6.9 cm long. (Collection of Her Majesty the Queen).

Fabergé's disinclination to only employ the usual costly materials of his profession led him to concentrate on the very varied mineral resources of the Urals, the Caucasus, and Siberia. The most typical stones he used were the following: nephrite (a spinach-green type of jade), bowenite (a pale-green, milky serpentine), rock crystal, the different varieties of agate (including chalcedony), jasper (including the green Kalgan type), rhodonite (a pink marble), obsidian (a dark-grey volcanic glass with velvety reflections), aventurine (a green, brown, or more rarely blue or black quartz with gold flecks that has been imitated by glassmakers), lapis-lazuli (a blue stone with gold spangles of pyrites), and purpurine (a purple vitreous material already known in the 18th century and rediscovered by Petouchov at the Imperial Glass Factory—used exclusively in the Fabergé workshop.) Fabergé knew how to make the most of the colours and decorative qualities of these stones in his designs.

Almost all the carved-stone pieces are unsigned, and the only guarantees of authenticity are either comparison with pieces known to have been purchased from Fabergé or the general quality of the workmanship, for example in the precision of the carving: on the animal figures this can be seen in the detailing of the fur or feathers, on the flowers in the thinness of the leaves (compare Plates 109 and 162).

Most of the stone articles stamped on one or another of their metal parts bear the mark of Henrik Wigström. This does not mean that they were actually made by Wigström himself, but that he supervised their manufacture and assembly.

The Animals. A feature of Fabergé animal carvings is the care with which the stone was selected to match as faithfully as possible the colouring of the creature concerned. The artist exploited the natural properties of the material, just as the ancient gem-carvers did, to get even closer to what he was representing—using, for example, the stripes in certain types of agate to imitate the tiger's markings.

Fabergé's animal world offers both naturalism and caricature. In the former case the modeller, and after him the carver, stayed as close as possible to the original. Often only a few centimetres high, these animal carvings are amazingly accurate right down to the last detail. In the case of caricatures there is an extra, humorous dimension, not just in the outward shape of the figure but also in the choice of stone: purple elephants and navy-blue rabbits anticipate the world of Walt Disney (Plate 100).

The Sandringham menagerie (in the collection of Her Majesty the Queen) born of Queen Alexandra's love of animals, is purely naturalistic. Her liking for the work of Fabergé (plate 107) was well known among her circle of friends, who were happy to delight her with small, not-too-expensive presents from the firm's London shop (Plates 158–9). One day Mrs George Keppel, a close friend of the royal family, had the idea of getting Fabergé to do the Queen's particular favourites, such as her dogs and the Derby winner, Persimmon. The King, however, wanted the entire contents of the farmyard as well: cows and bulls, hens and cockerels, turkeys, ducks, horses, and pigs. Modellers from St. Petersburg—including Boris Froedman-Cluzel and the Swiss Frank Lutiger—were dispatched to England post-haste to make models secretly from the life. The King gave his agreement to the models at Sandringham on 8 December 1907, and they were then sent to Fabergé's workshop in St. Petersburg to be carved in stone. The carvings—technically and artistically perfect—were sent back to London, where the King purchased them all. From then on, friends of the royal family made it their business to add to the menagerie each year (Plate 105) and when, following the outbreak of the First World War, the London shop had to close, the Royal Collection numbered more than 350 animals.

Other Fabergé enthusiasts followed the royal example. One of them was Léopold de Rothschild, who had his animals—mainly the racehorses—depicted in a similar fashion.

The Flowers. Among the most beautiful products of Fabergé's hardstone and goldsmiths' workshops are the small sprays of flowers in vases. These continued an old Russian tradition; diamond-studded model flowers dating from the 18th century can still be admired today in the Hermitage and Kremlin Armoury museums.

The Russian winter is long and monotonous, so that particular importance attaches to the first signs of spring. For a Russian, flowers are a symbol of good luck and of the renewal of hope. Special trains used to bring spring flowers on ice from the Crimea and the south of France to decorate court balls and private houses. In a country where nature is in bloom for a few months only, Fabergé's 'everlasting' flowers were highly popular. Particularly at Easter time the ladies of St. Petersburg society received presents of Fabergé flowers.

Realism was the key-note here, and Fabergé used every means at his disposal to make his flowers imitate nature. He began with a small, transparent vase of rock crystal, carved to look as if it contained water. In rarer cases these vases were made of semi-precious stones—agate, jasper or lapis-lazuli, simulating flower-pots or tubs (Plate 111). The stems and leaf stalks were done in gold, finely chased; the leaves were usually nephrite; the flowers and fruit were executed in coloured stones, often enamelled and set with pearls and diamonds. Fabergé created some masterpieces of naturalism—such as the moss (Plate 112), made of gold thread and platinum fibres adorning the famous basket of lilies-of-the-valley, or the ethereal dandelion seed-clock made of asbestos fibre, platinum, and rose diamonds, or the bouquet of cornflowers and buttercups, complete with a bee (Collection of Her Majesty, the Queen Mother).

The Figures. In the annals of hardstone carving Fabergé's composite stone figures, above all those illustrating the different types of Russian national costume, occupy a very special place. Only some thirty of these figures are known, which puts them among the rarest objects in the entire Fabergé œuvre[24].

The technique of fitting together different sorts of stone in a variety of colours had its culmination in 17th-century Florence. Fabergé was undoubtedly familiar, from his travels as a student, with the work of the *Opificio delle pietre dure* (the Medici's hardstone-carving workshop in Florence), and with the magnificent table tops and composite hardstone figures in the Palazzo Pitti and in the Hermitage. Using the technique he had studied there, Fabergé produced technically perfect figures in deliberate polychromy representing characters from the everyday life of St. Petersburg. We find the Tsar's mother's bodyguard (which Tsar Nicholas II commissioned together with other Cossack figures to give to his mother) the street vendors, balalaika players, *boyars,* workmen, soldiers, coachmen, peasants—right down to the House of Fabergé's factotum caretaker complete with broom, apron and cap (Plate 113). The realism of these figures makes it easy to dismiss them as *kitsch,* although this tradition, employed by Fabergé, dates back to the 18th century.

109 Three different wild flowers *(left to right):* Marsh-marigold of gold and yellow enamel with nephrite leaves, 14.5 cm high. Enamelled cornflower with diamond pistils and gold stem in a rock-crystal vase, 11.4 cm high. Buttercup of enamelled gold in a rock-crystal vase, 8.3 cm high, workmaster Henrik Wigström. (Formerly Robert Strauss Collection).

110 Lily-of-the-valley made of pearls, gold and nephrite and set with rose-diamonds, in a rock-crystal vase, 17.8 cm high. (Formerly Robert Strauss Collection).

111 Wild rose made of gold, white enamel and nephrite and set with diamonds, in a tub of pale jade on a Japanese-style base, 17.8 cm high, gold mark 72, workmaster Henrik Wigström. This is a documentary piece illustrating the influence of Japanese art on Fabergé.

112 Basket of lilies-of-the-valley. The flowers have pearl and rose-diamond buds, gold stalks and nephrite leaves; the gold basket has a cushion of moss in green gold and platinum fibres, 19 cm high, workmaster August Holmström, before 1895. The basket was presented by the merchants of Nishnj Novgorod to Tsarina Alexandra Feodorovna on the occasion of her coronation in 1896. It stood on her desk until 1917 (cf. *Stolitsa i Usadba,* 1914, Biblio. no. 24). A dedication is inscribed underneath the basket. This is one of Fabergé's most famous masterpieces. (The Matilda Geddings Grey Foundation Collection, New Orleans).

113 Three hardstone figures: *(top)* a soldier of the Preobrashenski guards regiment: nephrine uniform, obsidian boots, aventurine quartz face and hands, cabochon sapphire eyes, 12.7 cm high, signed under the right boot. (Collection of Mrs. Josiane Woolf); a Chelsea pensioner, 12 cm high, mentioned in the sales ledger of Fabergé's London branch: as sold on 22 November 1909 to 'H. M. the King, Model of a Chelsea Pensioner in pour-pourine, black onyx, silver, enl. 2 sapphires, no. 18913, £49/15/- ($240).' (Collection of Her Majesty the Queen).
(bottom) Fabergé's caretaker *(dvornik):* lapis-lazuli shirt, obsidian waistcoat, white quartz apron, obsidian cap with silver-gilt badge inscribed 'Dvornik, 24 Morskaya', gold broom, 12.8 cm high, signed, St. Petersburg, 1899–1908 (Formerly collection of Sir William Seeds).

114 Hardstone figure of a street vendor of woollen wares (trousers, socks, shawls and cloths), 13 cm high. This figure, which we are publishing for the first time, shows all the virtuosity of Fabergé's hardstone-cutting workshop. The shawls and cloths are in quartz, lapis-lazuli, orletz (a type of rhodonite) and nephrite; they are inset with borders and bands in hardstones of other colours.

115 Examples of jewellery *(left to right):* Gold and amethyst brooch, mounted in silver, rose-diamond setting, 3.5 cm wide, signed with initials; gold-mounted brooch with an octagonal emerald surrounded by rose-diamonds and fourteen circular-cut diamonds, 4.5 cm wide, signed with initials; gold-mounted sapphire brooch, inset with diamonds, 3.5 cm wide, workmaster August Holmström. The unusual quality of the stones in these brooches leads one to think that they may have been special commissions.

Precious Stones and Jewellery

Fabergé's concept of manufacturing ornamental art objects whose value was to lie in their decorativeness and workmanship rather than in their intrinsic commercial value also influenced his use of precious stones for such objects. He tended to confine himself to rose-diamonds and such coloured stones as emeralds, sapphires, and rubies *en cabochon* (i. e. polished but not shaped or faceted). Brilliant-cut diamonds are relatively rare on Fabergé articles, though they were used occasionally on pieces commissioned by the Tsar. Rose-diamonds and cabochons suited Fabergé's purpose better in that they remain a subordinate element in the overall decorative design of a piece, whereas brilliants, by catching the eye, tend to have a distracting effect. Fabergé's use of table-cut or 'portrait' diamonds for covering dates or initials should also be mentioned in this respect (Plate 136).

It was also due to Fabergé's basic affinity for ornamental art objects that the St. Petersburg firm particularly dealt so little in pure jewellery items such as diamond necklaces and tiaras. Usually the workshops only produced that kind of thing when commissioned to do so (Plate 115). Fabergé quite consciously saw himself as having little in common with the major French jewellery firms of Cartier, Boucheron, and the American Tiffany[25]. Jewellery for him meant an artistic ornamental object that could be worn about the person. Consequently we find a great many brooches, pendants for chains, and tie pins, decorated with enamel and with just a few (often tiny) precious stones. Apart from the many Easter-egg pendants (Plate 124), the brooches with the Russian imperial crown or the Monomach crown (which the Tsarina designed herself) were equally famous.

In these small, unobtrusive pieces of jewellery Fabergé often combined rose-diamonds with semiprecious stones, exhibiting a particular preference for what is called Mecca stone, a cabochon of artificially coloured chalcedony, ranging from pale blue to pale pink (Plate 85, third row).

Fabergé's Easter Eggs

Of all the age-old pagan symbols to have survived into our own day, the egg, symbol of creation and of life itself, is the one that springs most readily to mind. Under St. Augustine the pagan egg came to symbolize the Resurrection of Christ. In Europe, egg collecting and the giving of eggs at Easter date back to the Middle Ages. In Russia it has been customary since the dawn of Christianity to celebrate the Resurrection and the beginning of spring with the exchange of three kisses and the gift of an egg. The idea of dyeing eggs to make them more attractive evolved towards the end of the thirteenth century in Europe. Like so many countries, for centuries Russia has produced coloured natural Easter eggs—still the most common form of gift today. The practice of manufacturing artifical eggs did not, however, appear until the late eighteenth century. Eggs in glass or porcelain from the imperial factories of St. Petersburg, in hardstone from Ekatarinenburg, or in papier-mâché from Lukutin or Vishniakov were highly popular with the common people, while the aristocracy and the rich commissioned more elaborate examples in gold or silver and enamel, set with precious stones. Egg-shaped bonbonnières filled with sweets were great favourites.

The miniature Easter-egg pendant first appeared in the 18th century. Very rare diamond-set examples, a few of which may be seen in the Treasury of the Hermitage, served as prototypes for Fabergé, some of whose eggs were in fact direct copies of earlier examples. But it was Fabergé who made the miniature Easter egg so popular. These eggs and charms would be found dangling in large numbers from the necklaces and bracelets of all ladies of good society at Easter time, to be added to by every admirer, relative or friend. Some of these collections totalled up to one hundred examples. Only the most skilful craftsmen could use guilloché enamel and precious stones effectively on such small surfaces, while the tiny hardstone eggs carved in many shapes and colours called for the finest lapidaries. Fabergé's miniature Easter eggs leave us marvelling at their incredible diversity. They range from simple chased gold eggs to examples set with precious stones that form patterns, from monochrome guilloché eggs to those enamelled in various colours applied with emblems, from cheap hardstone eggs to eggs set with diamonds of quality, and they include egg-shaped charms in the form of animals, baskets of flowers, helmets, insects and crowns. Hardly ever are two pieces identical, despite the fact that they were produced by the thousand to meet the ever-growing demand preceding Easter (Plate 124).

Fabergé also produced egg-shaped functional objects as Easter presents, e. g. bonbonnières, bell pushes, flasks and seals, many examples of which can be seen in collections today. One example is a jasper bell push surmounted by an elephant; it is contained in the original painted wooden case in the shape of an Easter egg.[26]

The Imperial Easter Eggs

All these eggs herald chronologically the series of large Easter eggs commissioned by Tsars Alexander III and Nicholas II, which are without parallel in the history of applied art. Perhaps in connection with the imperial warrant received in 1884,

116   Easter egg, shaped as a basket of flowers and profusely set with diamonds, 2 cm high, probably by the French jeweller Boucheron, dated 1901. This is a highly instructive example of the influence of Fabergé's imperial Easter eggs, following their showing at the 1900 World Fair in Paris. (Collection of Her Majesty the Queen).

117   The Cartier Easter Egg, made of gold with purple guilloché enamel, diamonds and pearls on a pale green jade cushion. It opens to reveal a photograph of the tsarevitch, 9.5 cm high, made by Picq-Lavabre for Cartier and delivered to the City of Paris on 12 May 1918. The non-imperial crown, the misunderstanding of the imperial cypher and the photograph of the tsarevitch— probably the only one available in the West— would tend to show that this pastiche was made independently of actual Russian sources. (The Metropolitan Museum of Art, New York).

118–119   Two sketches in gouache colours for unrecorded Easter eggs by Hugo Oeberg: at the bottom of Pl. 118 are the initials A. F. for Agathon Fabergé; Pl. 119 shows an egg with signs of the Zodiac. These sketches are from the Fabergé family archives and are stamped with the Paris branch's archive mark.

116

117

118

119

120

121

122

123

120 Egg-shaped incense-burner of enamelled gold with a wide band of mauve guilloché enamel above and below, having decoration of scrolling foliage and putti. In the middle there is a wide band of *en plein* grisaille enamel, painted with an allegory of Catherine the Great's fame. In the sky, above the altar at which the peoples of Russia (in Roman dress) are sacrificing their hearts, the imperial monogram appears. Three hoof feet of chased gold are holding the incense-burner on a grey jasper base, 22 cm high, by Jean Jacques Duc, *c.* 1770. This Easter egg in the Hermitage, Leningrad, was made as a present for Catherine the Great and can be regarded as one of the sources for Fabergé's series of Easter eggs.

121 The Romanov Tercentenary Egg, presented by Tsar Nicholas II to his wife, Alexandra Feodorovna, in 1913. This gold egg with opalescent white enamel has an applied pattern of chased double-headed eagles and crowns, framing eighteen miniatures of Romanov rulers done by Zuiev; the purpurine base is surmounted by a double-headed eagle. The egg contains a parcel-gilt globe of blue steel in two halves, showing the boundaries of the Russian Empire in 1613 and in 1913, 18.6 cm high, workmaster Henrik Wigström, dated 1913. The egg was made to commemorate the tercentenary of Romanov rule in Russia. (Original Fabergé photograph; Armoury Museum, the Kremlin, Moscow).

122 The Danish Silver Jubilee Egg, presented by Tsar Alexander III to his wife, Marie Feodorovna, in 1888. This egg is made of gold with opalescent white and pale blue enamel; it is set with precious stones and contains a double-sided miniature screen, on which are portraits of King Christian IX and Queen Louise of Denmark,

25.4 cm high. It was given to the tsarina on the occasion of the Silver Jubilee of her father, the king of Denmark. (Original Fabergé photograph; present whereabouts unknown).

123 The Uspensky Cathedral Egg, presented by Tsar Nicholas II to his wife, Alexandra Feodorovna, in 1904; it is made of gold with white and green enamel; the egg is standing on an onyx base, 36.8 cm high, signed and dated on the base: Fabergé 1904. It represents the cupola of the Uspensky Cathedral, surrounded by the Kremlin's towers; through the windows of the cathedral, the frescoes and altar are visible. (Armoury Museum, the Kremlin, Moscow).

124 Collection of miniature Easter eggs (enlarged) made of gold, enamel and hardstone and set with diamonds, rubies and sapphires. Most of them are only signed with the workmaster's initials on the suspension ring.

125 The Alexander III Equestrian Egg, presented by Tsar Nicholas II to his mother, the Dowager Empress Marie Feodorovna, in 1910. This rock-crystal egg is mounted in platinum and set with rose-diamonds; it contains an equestrian figure of Tsar Alexander III in gold on a lapis-lazuli base, 13.5 cm high, signed in Cyrillic characters, dated 1910. It commemorates the unveiling in St. Petersburg in the same year of an equestrian figure of Alexander III made by Paul Troubetzkoi. (Armoury Museum, the Kremlin, Moscow).

126 The Coronation Coach Egg, presented by Tsar Nicholas II to his wife, Alexandra Feodorovna, in 1897. This gold egg with yellow enamel has an applied trellis pattern and double-

headed eagles in black enamel. It contains an exact replica in gold and strawberry enamel of the coronation coach; the miniature coach was made by George Stein. The egg's surface is decorated with motifs recalling the coronation robes used by the tsarina the previous year, 12.7 cm long, workmaster Michael Perchin, dated 1897. (The Forbes Collection, New York).

127 The Madonna-lily Clock Egg, presented by Tsar Nicholas II to his wife, Alexandra Feodorovna, in 1899, is made of gold with yellow guilloché enamel and set with rose-diamonds. It has a revolving dial of opaque white enamel with Roman numerals set in diamonds; it is surmounted by a bouquet of Madonna lilies made of quartzite and set with rose-diamonds, 26.7 cm high, workmaster Michael Perchin, 1889–1908. (Armoury Museum, the Kremlin, Moscow).

128 The Clover Egg, probably presented by Tsar Nicholas II to his wife, Alexandra Feodorovna, in 1902. Some of the clover leaves, made of chased gold and green *plique à jour* enamel, are set with rose-diamonds and decorated with a pattern of ribbons composed of calibrated rubies, 8.9 cm high, workmaster Michael Perchin. (Armoury Museum, the Kremlin, Moscow).

129 The Colonnade Egg, probably presented by Tsar Nicholas II to his wife, Alexandra Feodorovna, in 1905, the year following the tsarevitch's birth. This clock egg, shaped like a temple of love and made of bowenite, vari-coloured gold and pink enamel, has two platinum doves underneath the egg and four silver-gilt cherubs around the base, 28.6 cm high, workmaster Henrik Wigström. (Collection of Her Majesty the Queen).

Fabergé's firm was requested to make an egg for Tsar Alexander III as a present for the tsarina. The story goes that the tsar wished to give his wife Dagmar (born princess of Denmark) a very special Easter present to remind her of her Danish home. Fabergé's first imperial Easter egg (Cat. Plate 1) faithfully copies a similar egg of gold and opaque white enamel, containing a miniature hen; today it is still in Rosenborg Castle, Copenhagen.[27] The immediate success of this idea resulted in an imperial commission for a new Fabergé egg every year, each to contain some delightful surpirse; there followed the extraordinary series of imperial presentation Easter eggs by Fabergé, which surpassed anything hitherto seen in beauty and value.

Eleven of these eggs would seem to have been made for Tsar Alexander III between 1884/5 and 1894, the year of his death. His son Tsar Nicholas II continued the tradition by presenting both his mother, the dowager empress, and his wife Alexandra with such an egg for Easter from 1895 up to 1917, making another 46. Of the total of 57 eggs presumably made, all except for 11 are known to us in some form or another: ten of the eggs are still in Russia, jealously preserved in the Armoury Museum of the Kremlin. All the others have found their way to the West: 25 are in the United States including 9 in the Forbes Collection, New York; 7 of them are in Europe, and of the remaining 4 the present whereabouts are unknown.

Many problems arise, when examining these imperial Easter eggs in detail; of the 11 eggs made for Tsar Alexander III only four are dated. To start with, we only possess Eugène Fabergé's testimony that the first egg was made in 1884. The dating of the remainder varies from author to author and can only be arrived at by assumption, but it would seem logical to put the simplest and smallest eggs at the beginning. Of the 23 eggs supposedly presented by Tsar Nicholas II to his mother, 17 were thought to have been identified. On the basis of facts that have recently come to light (see Plate 141) this number must now be reduced by three, for these formed part of the series made for Barbara Kelch. Of the 23 eggs made for Tsarina Alexandra Feodorovna in the same years, specialists believe they have identified all but one (Cat. Plate 41); a closer look, however, shows that for at least five eggs the recipient is quite uncertain, and for four the date is equally unsure.

As in the case of most of Fabergé's art, the inspiration for these eggs comes from eighteenth-century prototypes. We may safely assume that Fabergé knew of earlier Easter eggs containing surprises (like those presented by Louis XV and Louis XVI to their family); two examples are still preserved today in the Musée Lambinet at Versailles.[28] The egg in Rosenborg Castle, according to Danish royal family tradition, also originates from 18th-century France.

It seems to have escaped notice up to now that sumptuous Easter eggs were also traditional in 18th-century Russia. Such eggs from the Imperial Collections, which would definitely have been known to Fabergé, may still be seen in the Treasury of the Hermitage. One example is an egg-shaped incense-burner of gold and pale lilac enamel, decorated with a grisaille painting glorifying Catherine the Great (Plate 120). It is the work of the well-known goldsmith Jean-Jacques Duc (active 1770–85). A set of seven gold-mounted Easter eggs, enamelled ivory, in the S. Niarchos Collection, Paris, undoubtedly served as models for one of the earliest imperial eggs by Fabergé. For the 1903 Peter the Great Egg (Plate 133), Fabergé was inspired by a Louis-XV gold Easter egg, containing a watch as a surprise, that is also in the Hermitage.[29] From the same source, Fabergé used the extraordinary peacock automaton by James Cox,[30] (a present from Potemkin to Catherine the Great) as a model for his 1908 Peacock Egg (Cat. Plate 25).

Definite proof of Fabergé's studies in the *Grünes Gewölbe* (Green Vaults) Collection in Dresden also exists in the form of a direct copy of an 18th-century casket by Le Roy of Amsterdam[31] and recognizable in the 1894 Renaissance Egg (Plate 137). Others have seen the Resurrection Egg (Cat. Plate 2) and the 1909 Standart Egg (Plate 135) as further copies from Dresden originals. As sources of inspiration for the Serpent Clock Egg (Cat. Plate 6) and the Orange Tree Egg (Plate 139), 18th-century French prototypes may safely be postulated.

The remainder of the imperial Easter eggs are very much Fabergé's own invention. All but a few have some sort of iconographic connection with the imperial family or with an historic Russian anniversary. They commemorate birthdays, trips or jubilees; they show miniatures of the various members of the family, their activities and their favourite palaces. And despite the fact that scholars have identified a number of originals as sources for Fabergé's eggs, his interpretation of the earlier prototypes remains highly personal.

Typically for this eclectic period preceding the art nouveau style, the eggs vary in style: some adopt the idiom of the Renaissance, a few are baroque (or rather Louis XV) interpretations, while many follow a Louis XVI vocabulary. As the series of eggs advances, however, the adaptation of these historical styles becomes freer. In the early 1890s, but more especially from 1897 onwards, Fabergé developed a personal style in which he made free use of stylistic elements from all periods, often combined simultaneously.

It should be added that each of the 46 eggs known is quite unique. Fabergé permitted himself no repetition when working on this most important commission from his imperial patrons. Pictures of the imperial Easter eggs make them appear to be large-scale works, and people are invariably surprised when confronted with their actual size, which is quite small. This effect of monumentality—achieved here on such small-scale objects—characterizes all great plastic art.

All the Easter eggs (but particularly those made between 1891 and 1914) are highly miniaturized, lavish productions, truly reflecting the wealth and splendour of the imperial court in those years. Each of these masterpieces tries to surpass its predecessor in invention, beauty and elegance. They constitute the last blossoming of European art in the service of great patrons. Each one is a masterpiece in itself, representing hundreds of hours of workmanship. All the workshops—those of the goldsmiths, enamellers, miniature painters, lapidaries and jewellers—collaborated to make them unique. Many of them conceal highly intricate mechanisms adapted from Swiss automatons. Thus the peacock in the Peacock Egg of 1908 (Cat. Plate 25), made by Dorofeiev, was the result of a number of reductions, starting with a life-sized model copied from Cox's automaton, until the miniature animal could be perfected——which according to Eugène Fabergé took three years. The coach in the Coronation Coach Egg of 1897 (Plate 126), by Georg Stein, took fifteen months to complete. Consequently Fabergé had to plan far ahead, as most of these elaborate works of art were several years in the making. From the first scale drawing embodying Fabergé's idea, right down to the specially constructed case, each step was controlled by the

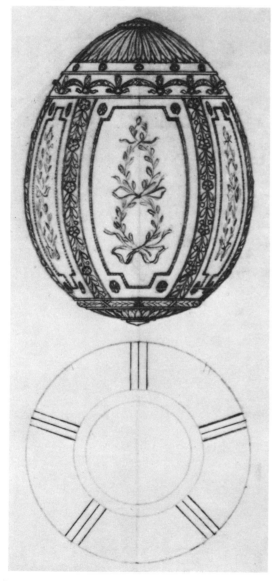

Rough pencil-drawing for an Easter egg from the Fabergé family archives, showing the idea for an Easter egg containing a basket of flowers.

master and thoroughly discussed at the round table with all the workmen concerned. Total secrecy surrounded the work. Not even the tsar was let in on the secret of the next year's surprise. The presentation of these eggs at court—up to 1894—was the responsibility of Carl Fabergé himself. During the reign of Tsar Nicholas II, Fabergé presented the egg to the tsarina, while the chief workmaster or Eugène Fabergé brought the tsar's present to his mother, the dowager empress.

Much as it started, the series finished on a subdued note. Following the outbreak of the First World War, the eggs made between 1915 and 1917 became much simpler, due to lack of funds. The materials chosen were cheaper—steel for the 1916 Military Egg (Cat. Plate 56) and apparently even wood for one of the 1917 eggs.

One egg from the imperial series—the Nicholas II Equestrian Egg of 1913 (Cat. Plate 65), commemorating the Romanov Tercentenary—was, according to tradition, a present from Tsarina Alexandra Feodorovna to her husband Tsar Nicholas II; it is apparently the only one of its kind.[32] Of lime-green enamel embellished with a diamond-set double-headed eagle and a miniature of the tsarina, this egg opens to reveal an equestrian portrait of the tsar.

The Non-imperial Eggs

In the land of Easter eggs *par excellence* it is quite logical that other very wealthy persons should have wished to emulate the members of the imperial family in their lavish Easter presents. One such man was the Siberian gold magnate and millionnaire Alexander Ferdinadovitch Kelch, who presented his wife Barbara, née Bazanov, with a series of Easter eggs as sumptuous as those of the tsars between 1898 and 1904 (Cat. Plates 58–64). Four of these eggs were previously been identified by the initials BK, which they bore. One of them, the first of the Kelch series (quite appropriately also a hen egg, Cat. Plate 58é) has since lost these initials. From the archives of what was originally 'A la Vieille Russie', an antique shop in Paris opened by Zolotnitzky of Kiev in 1921, a set of photographs (Plate 141) has recently come to light showing seven eggs acquired by him from the firm of Morgan, rue de la Paix, in 1920. Notes made by Zolotnitzky's nephew Léon Grinberg in 1922, provide proof that Alexander Fabergé identified six as having been made for Kelch—the seventh being the Nobel Ice Egg[33] (Plate 141, Cat. Plate 69). A newcomer to the Kelch series, as a result, is the Pine Cone Egg (Cat. Plate 60) of 1900[34] presumed by some to have been given to Marie Feodorovna (who was a Danish princess by birth) because of the Danish elephant it contains. According to Grinberg's notes this egg originally bore the Kelch initials under the portrait diamond. The other two eggs identified by Alexander Fabergé as belonging to the Kelch series are the Apple Blossom Egg[35] (Cat. Plate 61, dated 1901 by both Eugène and Alexander Fabergé) and the Chanticleer Egg (Plate 143, probable date 1904), both associated with the dowager empress.

Circumstantial evidence as to their non-imperial provenance is to be found in their similarity to other imperial eggs already in existence: as previously stated, Fabergé never produced two eggs even vaguely similar for his imperial patrons. On the other hand, when working for others he frequently copied existing models of his own, since there had to be bounds even to his extraordinary inventiveness.

130 The Winter Egg, presented by Tsar Nicholas II to his mother, Marie Feodorovna, in 1913. The egg, carved from a block of rock crystal applied with diamonds, stands on a rock-crystal base that simulates a slab of ice. It contains a basket of platinum and rose-diamonds that holds snowdrops made of olivine and nephrite, 10.2 cm high, engraved with the signature and date 1913. (Present whereabouts unknown).

131 The Gatchina Palace Egg, presented by Tsar Nicholas II to his mother, Marie Feodorovna, probably in 1902. This gold egg has a white guilloché enamel covering, painted with emblems, ribbons and swags and inset bands of seed pearls. It opens to reveal a model of Gatchina Palace in four-colour gold, 12.8 cm high, workmaster Michael Perchin. Gatchina Palace was the dowager empress's favourite residence. (The Walters Art Gallery, Baltimore).

132 The Napoleonic Egg, presented to the Dowager Empress Marie Feodorovna by her son, Tsar Nicholas II. Made of gold with green and red guilloché enamel and set with rose-diamonds, this egg contains a screen with six miniatures by Zuiev, showing members of the regiments of which the dowager empress was honorary colonel, 11.6 cm high, dated 1912, workmaster Henrik Wigström. It commemorates the 100th anniversary of the Russian wars of liberation, waged against Napoleon. (The Matilda Geddings Grey Foundation Collection, New Orleans).

133 The Peter the Great Egg, presented to the Tsarina Alexandra Feodorovna by her husband, Tsar Nicholas II, in 1903. This gold egg, chased with palm-leaves and scrolls and set with rose-diamonds, contains two enamel paintings by Zuiev, showing the house of Peter the Great and the Winter Palace. It also contains a miniature replica, modelled by Malychev, of Falconet's monument to Peter the Great that is in St. Petersburg, 15 cm high, workmaster Michael Perchin, dated 1903. This egg commemorates the bicentenary of the founding of St. Petersburg by Peter the Great. Fabergé clearly followed the model of a Louis XV-style clock in egg shape, in the Hermitage in Leningrad. (The Lillian Thomas Pratt Collection, Virginia Museum of Fine Arts, Richmond).

134 The Grisaille Egg, presented by Tsar Nicholas II to his mother, Marie Feodorovna, in 1914. It is made of gold and decorated with eight panels in grisaille and translucent pink, depicting the Muses and done by Zuiev, 12.5 cm high, workmaster Henrik Wigström, dated 1914. (Collection of Mrs. Marjorie Merriweather Post: the Hillwood Collection, Washington, D.C.).

135 The Standart Egg, presented by Tsar Nichoals II to his wife, Alexandra Feodorovna, probably in 1909. This egg has a gold-mounted shell of rock crystal that is enamelled and rests on a double-dolphin base of lapis-lazuli; the double-headed eagle handles are also in lapis-lazuli and hold hanging pearls. The egg contains a gold model of the imperial yacht Standart, placed on a block of aquamarine, simulating the sea, 13.7 cm high, workmaster Henrik Wigström. (Armoury Museum, the Kremlin, Moscow).

136 The Mosaic Egg, presented to Tsarina Alexandra Feodorovna by her husband, Tsar Nicholas II, in 1914, is composed of a platinum set with a network of calibrated diamonds, sapphires, rubies, emeralds, topazes and garnets forming a floral pattern. It contains a gold pedestal, decorated with pearls and diamonds, on which are miniatures of the tsarina's children painted in sepia grisaille, 9.2 cm high, engraved with Fabergé's name, made by August Holmström. (Collection of Her Majesty the Queen).

137 The Renaissance Egg, presented by Tsar Alexander III to his wife, Marie Feodorovna, in 1894. It is oval and made of milky opaque agate with enamelled gold mounts, 13.5 cm long, signed and dated 1894, workmaster Michael Perchin. This egg is an exact copy of an early 18th-century jewel casket by Le Roy of Amsterdam in the Green Vaults (*Grünes Gewölbe)* Collection in Dresden, East Germany. (The Forbes Collection, New York).

138 The Swan Egg, probably presented by Tsar Nicholas II to his wife, Alexandra Feodorovna in 1906. This gold egg with mat mauve enamel is applied with ribbons in a trellis pattern and inset with rose diamonds. It contains a mechanical platinum swan, resting on an aquamarine that simulates water, 10 cm high. (Collection of the heirs of Maurice Sandoz, Musée de l'Horlogerie, Le Locle, Switzerland).

139 The Orange Tree Egg, presented by Tsar Nicholas II to his mother, Marie Feodorovna, in 1911 is made of nephrite, white quartz, gold and enamel and set with pearls, rubies and diamonds, 26.7 cm high, signed and dated 1911. The tree conceals a singing-bird automaton, which functions when a jewelled fruit is pressed. This egg is undoubtedly a free copy after an 18th-century French original, similar to the example from the collection of the Earl of Roseberry, Mentmore Towers. (The Forbes Collection, New York).

140 The Youssoupov Easter Egg. This gold egg, covered with translucent pink enamel, is a revolving clock and has a diamond-set XXV on it as well as four miniatures of the Youssoupov family, 24 cm high, signed. It was presented to Princess Zenaide Youssoupov by her husband Felix in 1907 on the occasion of their 25th wedding anniversary. (Collection of the heirs of Maurice Sandoz, Musée de l'Horlogerie, Le Locle, Switzerland).

On the whole, the non-imperial eggs are larger than their counterparts. Thus the Duchess of Marlborough Egg (Plate 142), an unashamed pastiche in pink of the blue Serpent Clock Egg (Cat. Plate 6), is also much larger than its prototype. Typically of Fabergé, however, although the eggs are very similar, they differ in many details. This egg of Fabergé's would seem to have been the most important commission by a foreign client acquired in Russia itself. It was made for Consuelo Vanderbilt, Duchess of Marlborough, shortly before her visit to St. Petersburg in 1902.

In Russia Fabergé's best non-imperial client, the family of Emmanuel Nobel, also commissioned an Easter egg known as the Nobel Ice Egg (Cat. Plate 69). With its frosted shell it follows the example of the imperial Winter Egg of 1913 (Plate 130) and may therefore safely be dated 1914–16. Last but not least in the series of these elaborate Easter presents stands the Youssoupov (20th-Wedding Anniversary) Egg of 1907 (Plate 140), which also reverts to the theme of the Serpent Clock Egg (Cat. Plate 6). With its nephrite shell and suspended miniatures, however, this egg differs quite considerably from the other examples.

Fabergé and his Competitors

The importance that the name of Fabergé has taken on in recent years tends to obscure the fact that he was not the only famous figure on the Russian art scene in his time. His work, like that of most artists, must be appreciated in the context of a large number of other jewellers, gold- and silversmiths, enamellers and lapidaries, vying with him for imperial and public favour.

Between 1842 and 1860 (and even until 1870 when Peter Carl took over) Gustav Fabergé's jewellery shop was by no means the leading one in St. Petersburg. His main competitors were Carl and Henrik Bolin from Sweden, who opened a shop in 1845 and became goldsmiths and jewellers to the imperial court soon afterwards. Most imperial commissions before 1870 went automatically to them, as did that for the magnificent ruby and diamond parure ordered by Tsar Alexander II for the wedding of his daughter Marie Alexandra with Alfred, Duke of Edinburgh, in 1874[36]. Bolin also produced articles of vertu and important silver pieces towards the turn of the century (Plate 144), the latter in a pronouncedly bourgeois and often heavily art-nouveau style.

During the third quarter of the 19th century the 'English Shop' of Nichols and Plinke (1810–79) was a favourite with the imperial court. Their output—as the name implies, in the English (Georgian) styles and of high quality—is recognizable in most cases by its refined taste and unusually heavy weight.

The firm of Sazikov founded in Moscow by Pavel Sazikov in 1793 obtained the imperial warrant for Moscow in 1846 and for St. Petersburg in 1857. The St. Petersburg branch, directed from 1842 onwards by Valentin Sazikov and active until about 1882, specialized in silverware in the Russian taste.

The best-known Russian silversmith and enameller, Pavel Ovchinnikov,[37] opened his factory for gold and silverware in Moscow in 1853. It would seem that the introduction of what is today called the pan-Slavic style, harking back to the period of Peter the Great, was due to him. In 1873, only three years after Fabergé's start, Ovchinnikov also founded a branch in St. Petersburg. Ovchinnikov and Ivan Chlebnikov (established in St. Petersburg until 1867 and in Moscow from 1870), who also catered to the rich and traditionalist circles of society, both worked in the style mentioned above, which was sponsored by Tsar Alexander III and officially sanctioned by the pan-Russian Exhibitions of 1882 in Moscow and 1896 in Nishnj-Novgorod. For their exhibits in this 'retrospective' style both Ovchinnikov and Chlebnikov received the imperial warrant.

Specialists generally assume that between 1870 and 1884 Fabergé specialized in jewellery, whereas after his success at the Exhibition of 1882, he concentrated on *objets de fantaisie*. The workshop of August Holmström worked in the Empire style, producing elegant necklaces that differed considerably from the work of contemporary jewellers. Erik Kollin, head workmaster between 1870 and 1886, made gold objects in an archaizing style reminiscent of archeological finds and much in fashion everywhere else at that time, although without precedent in Russia. Kollin's art heralds the *objets de fantaisie* for which Fabergé was to become justly famous.

The turning point in Fabergé's career (between 1882 and 1884) coincides with his younger brother Agathon's entry into the firm, and with the success of their new *objets de vertu* in gold and enamel, exhibited at the pan-Russian Exhibition. There followed an ever-increasing output of objects of unsurpassed quality, which was without parallel in Russian art.

Fabergé introduced his personal style of ribbed cigarette cases in varicoloured gold, an immediate success that became a hallmark of his house. Further innovations were his functional objects for ladies, such as powder compacts, lipstick tubes, bonbonnières, scent bottles, fans, frames, cane and parasol handles, and objects for use by gentlemen in their offices such as clocks, frames, paper-knives, stamp wetters, gum-pots, cigar cases or cigarette boxes, seals and calendars.

Also without parallel in Russian art were the little flowers, hardstone animals, figures and miniature toys and furniture made for the decoration of the houses of the rich.

All these objects put Fabergé into a class of his own, and up until the turn of the century this aspect of Fabergé's art was to remain without competition. As Fabergé's work became the craze of St. Petersburg and the whole of Europe, many local artists (and even some major firms in France) envied his fame and tried to emulate him in both choice of form and style.

Karl Gustavovitch Hahn (or Ghan in Russian) may be regarded without doubt as Fabergé's most important competitor and by imperial appointment his equal. After Bolin, Hahn was the leading jeweller during the last decades of Romanov rule. The imperial family commissioned him to make the diadem that Tsarina Alexandra Feodorovna wore at her coronation in 1896, a magnificent pearl and diamond *kokoshnik*-shaped crown as shown on the portrait in the Hillwood Collection.[38] (The *kokoshnik* is a Russian woman's traditional, high headdress.) Hahn was also chosen to execute a lavish commemorative Tercentenary triptych for the imperial family (Plate 147), as well as numerous other objects for imperial presentation. The quality of his work, most of it dating from after 1900, is always excellent; however, the style is very different from that of Fabergé. Hahn's objects are more traditional, more ostentatious and more dependent on precious stones. They lack the elegance, lightness and charm of Fabergé's art. Moreover Hahn uses a palette of enamel colours—grey, salmon, steel-blue—that is totally different from Fabergé's; in many cases we find a juxtaposition of hues unmistakably his own (Plate 145). His objects are always stamped with his initial and name in Cyrillic characters.

Alexander Tillander and another workmaster signing S. W. in Cyrillic characters both also worked for Hahn. Tillander is often confused with Fabergé's workmaster Alfred Thielemann owing to the identity of initials. Their work is easily distinguished: Thielemann produced jewellery, Tillander *objets de vitrine* in the style of Fabergé. Tillander very often enamelled his frames and cigarette cases in a striking scarlet colour (Plate 146). Workmanship and style both differ from similar objects by Fabergé.

Among Fabergé's other competitors, Ivan Britzin takes a special place. Trained by Fabergé, Britzin closely followed the example of his master in his later *objets de vertu* (Plate 144). In recent years many examples of his frames and cigarette cases have appeared on the market. Lacking the quality of Fabergé's work—mostly pale blue or white, grey-blue, more rarely pale green, with rather wide borders or mounts, often

141   Objects illustrated on two pages of the archive album of 'A la Vieille Russie', Paris, dating from the 1920s, showing the Easter eggs purchased by this firm in 1920. With the exception of the Nobel Ice Egg (second from the bottom on the right), these eggs were all presented by the gold-mining magnate Kelch to his wife Barbara between 1898 and 1904.

142   The Duchess of Marlborough (Pink Serpent Clock) Egg. This gold egg is covered with pink guilloché enamel and has applied swags of varicoloured gold; the indicator is shaped like a serpent and set with diamonds. It stands on a triangular base with white enamel panels, one of which is decorated with the diamond-set crowned monogram CM, 23.5 cm high, signed, workmaster Michael Perchin. This egg was acquired by the Duchess of Marlborough (the former Consuelo Vanderbilt) during her visit to St. Petersburg in 1902. (The Forbes Collection, New York).

143   The Chanticleer Egg, made for Barbara Kelch, presumably in 1903 (the year of Perchin's death) for presentation in 1904. This egg is gold and covered with blue guilloché enamel; the Louis XVI-style base is in blue and white enamel, 27.5 cm high, signed, workmaster Michael Perchin. The egg contains a singing-bird automaton that functions every hour (see also Pl. 157 for an imperial Easter egg with a comparable mechanism). (The Forbes Collection, New York).

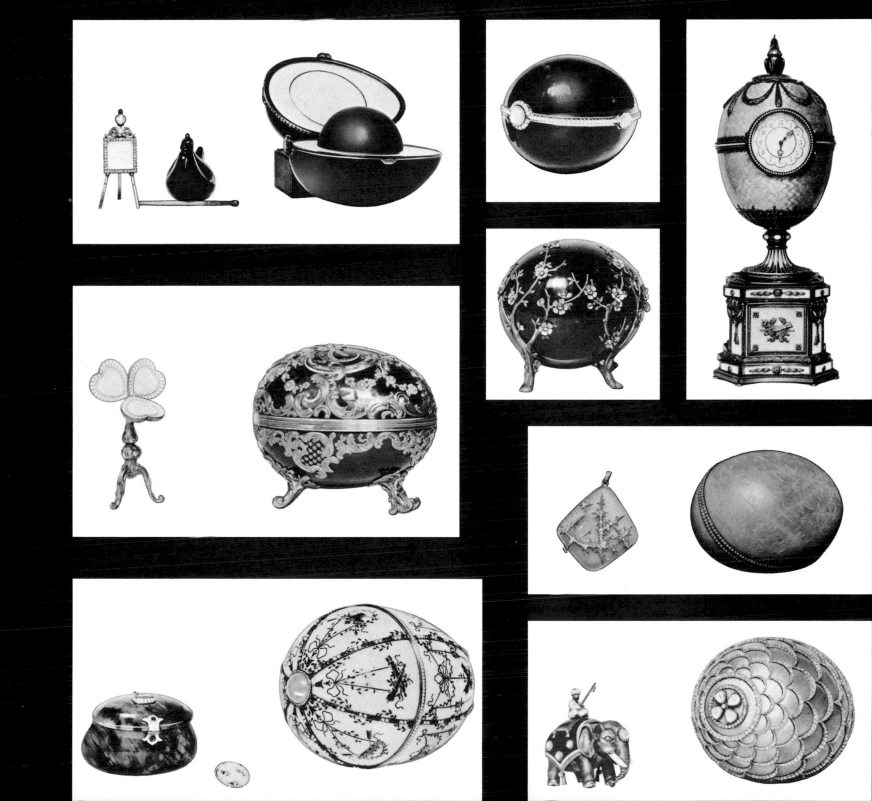

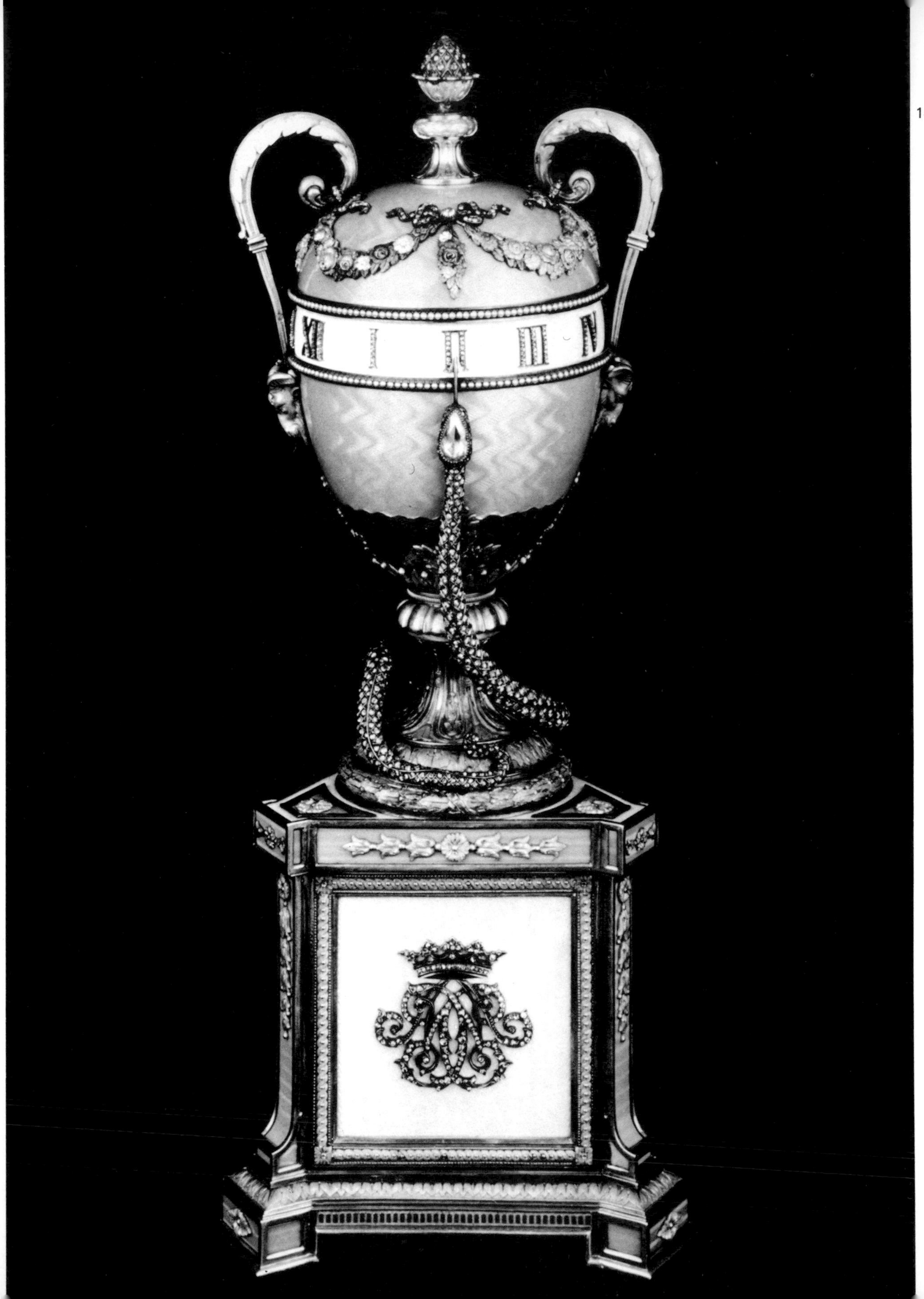

combining wood and gilded silver—his work is stamped either with his initials or with his initial and name in Cyrillic characters. His maple-wood cases are clear copies of Fabergé's: their lining bears a mark similar to his.

Two other competitors, A. I. Sumin and the firm of Astreyden in St. Petersburg, also copied Fabergé's art. Sumin produced mostly clocks, cigarette cases and frames, which can be found occasionally in cardboard boxes, marked with his initial and full name in Cyrillic characters. Sumin used the same colour-scheme as Britzin, with a predilection for white enamel and the occasional unexpected turquoise (Plate 144). Many objects, including white enamel cigarette and pencil cases and miniature Easter eggs in pale pink, yellow, mauve and blue are stamped A. A., presumably standing for Astreyden, who seems to have had a working relationship with Sumin. The Third *Artel* (cooperative of gold- and silversmiths in St. Petersburg following in Fabergé's footsteps) is also closely connected with Sumin and Astreyden. Their mark 3A often identifies clocks or frames in Fabergé's style and colour but quite frequently also in non-Fabergé colours such as deep raspberry. It would seem that Sumin and the jeweller Denissov-Ouralski both also made hardstone objects imitating Fabergé.

Fabergé's popular cigarette cases found imitators in Fritz Koechli (mark F. K., with a star between the initials, or his full name in Cyrillic characters), Marshak and Morosov (both of whose marks were full names in Cyrillic characters).

Some Russian firms like Marshak of Kiev and Bolin of Moscow named temporary representatives in Paris; others like Fabergé sent salesmen from London to Paris, the Côte d'Azur and Rome. Similarily the Paris firms of Cartier and Boucheron vied with their Russian competitors in their own country. Both sent representatives regularly to Russia with a selection of their finest jewellery, the former at Easter, the latter at Christmas.

Cartier's named a correspondent in St. Petersburg in 1902, the same person who represented the high-fashion dress designer Worth. Louis Cartier visited St. Petersburg himself in 1910 at the invitation of Grand Duchess Maria Pavlovna, his patron, and there he met Fabergé. Cartier's work was in high demand in Russia right up until the First World War: at the Youssoupov wedding in 1914, for instance, the majority of the jewellery came from Cartier's.

Boucheron, advised by Bolin, opened a branch office in Moscow in the last years of the 19th century under the direction of a Mr. Delavigne. A large number of Bolin's rich clients, such as the oil magnates Nobel, lived in the Caucasus from where they regularly sent very important commissions. Hoping to obtain some for Boucheron and not deterred by Bolin's descriptions of banditism in the provinces, Mr. Delavigne and his well-armed son travelled southwards by train with a selection of choice jewels. Both were robbed and murdered in their compartment, setting a premature end to Boucheron's Russian enterprise.

Both Cartier and Boucheron produced imitations of the Fabergé's work that was exhibited in Paris at the World Fair of 1900 (Plates 116, 117).

Collectors and Collections

Before 1917

It should be noted that before 1917 there were no 'collectors' of Fabergé, as most of his objects were considered purely functional. Bainbridge says of this period, 'Except in rare cases I never remember the Edwardian ladies buying anything for themselves; they received their Fabergé objects as gifts from men, and these gifts were purely for the psychological moment'.[39] The largest Fabergé collection of all time, that of the master's imperial patrons, which must have numbered in the thousands, has been dispersed by the Soviet government and can now be found oceans away. Apart from the 10 imperial Easter eggs that can be viewed in the Armoury museum in the Kremlin today, very little of Fabergé's work remains in the Soviet Union.

Other private collections formed before the Russian Revolution left the country with their owners, who all emigrated. Such was the case of the collection of Emmanuel Nobel, whom Fabergé considered his most important non-aristocratic patron. Nobel purchased many hundreds of pieces, including a whole series of hardstone figures to adorn his table when guests were invited. Like the imperial family, the Nobels were in the habit of giving small objects by Fabergé at Easter and other feasts. The Kelchs were also assiduous collectors of Fabergé's work, though only the six Easter eggs can be connected with them. Othmar Neuscheller, owner of a rubber factory, and his in-laws, the van der Pals, also belonged to Fabergé's faithful clientèle; both families acquired numerous pieces of jewellery and enamelled objects.[40]

Possibly Fabergé's first English clients in Russia were the Duchess of Marlborough who is known to have acquired the pink Serpent Clock Egg (Plate 142) in St. Petersburg in 1902, Lady Diana Cooper and Lady Sackville of whom Bainbridge wrote, 'She was, I think, as much of an inspiration to Fabergé as he was to her'. Both the latter travelled to Russia and returned 'laden with treasures from Fabergé'.

Another early collector of Fabergé was Mr Walters of Baltimore, who purchased a number of hardstone animals in St. Petersburg in 1900, when he stopped there with his yacht. Walters later purchased two imperial Easter eggs, which are on view with his collection in the Walters Art Gallery, Cleveland[41] (Plate 131, Cat. Plate 47).

In London Fabergé's clients included all of Edwardian society, led by the King and Queen. The English royal family today owns the largest collection of objects by Fabergé (some 450 pieces in all) many of which were exhibited for the first time in 1977 at the Victoria and Albert Museum.

Other great collections were formed during this period—such as the one of Grand Duke Michael Mikhailovitch, inherited by the late Lady Zia Wernher of Luton Hoo, and that of the English branch of the Rothschild family, which acquired and commissioned several hundred Fabergé pieces between 1907 and 1917.

Many royal families in Europe that are related to the Russian imperial family, such as the Houses of Denmark, Greece, Rumania, Bulgaria and a number of German royal families still retain much of what they received before the Russian Revolution. Hundreds of Fabergé objects, since inherited by second or third generations, are still treasured in private and remain hidden from the public eye.

145 Presentation snuffbox made of gold with grey and pale pink guilloché enamel and set with gems; the lid has an applied double-headed eagle inset with diamonds and rubies, 7 cm across, signed Hahn (in Cyrillic characters), workmaster S.W., St. Petersburg, 1899–1908. Tsar Nicholas II presented this snuffbox to the Persian Viceroy. It is a typical example of the art of Fabergé's main competitor Hahn, which differs in many ways from his own, for example in the profusion of precious stones.

146 A frame of gold and scarlet guilloché enamel, 7.6 cm high, signed with the initials of Alexander Tillander, St. Petersburg, before 1899.

147 The Romanov tercentenary triptych is made of gold and blue guilloché enamel; diamond-set monograms of Tsar Nicholas II and his wife, Alexandra Feodorovna, are applied on a white ground with the dates 1613 and 1913 and a double-headed eagle. The triptych opens to reveal miniatures of the tsar, the tsarina and the tsarevitch, 14 cm high, imperial warrant mark of K.K. Hahn. This is apparently the most important commision received by Fabergé's main competitor, Hahn. (The Forbes Collection, New York).

148 A frame of gold and white guilloché enamel with a green border, inset with rose-diamonds and pearls and containing a miniature portrait (by Zuiev) of the wife of the rubber factory owner, Othmar Neuscheller, 20.1 cm high, signed, workmaster Henrik Wigström, 1899–1908.

149 The Coronation Box is made of gold and yellow guilloché enamel; double-headed eagles in black enamel are applied to the box with rose-diamonds and the cypher of Tsar Nicholas II, 9.5 cm long, signed, workmaster August Holmström, St. Petersburg, before 1899. Presented by Tsarina Alexandra Feodorovna to her husband Tsar Nicholas II in 1897, the year after their coronation. (The Forbes Collection, New York).

145

146

147

JVNE
XXII
MCMXI

150 The 'Balletta' Box is a vanity case in gold and blue enamel, decorated with trellis work and the monogram E. B. in rose-diamonds; the reverse is in *basse-taille* enamel with floral swags and has the crowned initial A. The interior contains a gold pencil, an ivory tablet, a mirror, a lipstick tube and two compartments for powder, 10 cm long, signed, workmaster Henrik Wigström. This vanity case was presented by Grand Duke Alexei Alexandrovitch to the famous actress Elizabeth Balletta of the Imperial Michael Theatre in St. Petersburg. The Grand Duke, whose monogram appears on the base, was brother of Tsar Alexander III and admiral-in-chief of the Russian navy. He was a great admirer of the fair sex, and it was said of him that he preferred 'slow ships and fast women'. Mrs. Balletta emigrated to Paris with her collection of Fabergé objects (for the most part presents from her various royal admirers); there she slowly disposed of them.

151 Rock-crystal vase mounted on enamelled gold and set with gems, 16.5 cm high, workmaster Michael Perchin. It was presented by Leopold de Rothschild to Queen Mary of England on the occasion of her coronation in 1911. The vase was filled with orchids from Rothschild's hothouse when it was presented. In the sales ledger of Fabergé's London branch, it is mentioned as 'Leopold de Rothschild: Cup, rock-crystal eng., gold 72°, en diff. stones, no. 8011, nett £430/-/- ($2,100)'. (Collection of Her Majesty the Queen).

152 Rectangular silver cigarette box, gold-mounted and enamelled in the Rothschild racing colours—blue and yellow, 13.5 cm long, signed, workmaster Henrik Wigström. This is probably the box sold to Albert de Goldschmidt-Rothschild in London on 13 July 1913: 'Cig.tte Box, blue & yellow enal. stripes; gold mts, no. 20938, £ 125/-/- ($650)'.

After the closing down of Fabergé's shops late in 1918 and the end of Fabergé's production, serious 'collecting' began. One of the earliest collectors of the post-revolutionary period was A. E. Bradshaw, who acquired his entire collection from Wartski's in London. There was a time when he was the owner of some 20 hardstone Russian figures, several imperial Easter eggs, some hundreds of animal sculptures, and a large quantity of enamel wares. The entire Bradshaw collection has been dispersed over the years.

After 1924, when the Soviet Union resumed diplomatic relations with the West, some foreign envoys in Moscow also formed important collections. The French ambassador Jean Herbette (in Moscow from 1924–30) and his wife are an example. Their vast Russian collection, including many objects by Fabergé, was sold in Geneva in 1970–1. Marjorie Merriweather Post (attached to the American embassy in Moscow from 1936 to 1938) was also introduced to Fabergé's art there and as a result formed an important collection of Russian art that includes two imperial Easter eggs and is on view today at the Hillwood Collection in Washington, D. C.[38] (Plate 134, Cat. Plate 9).

Matilda Geddings Grey began collecting in 1933 after a visit to the Chicago Century of Progress Exhibition, where she met Dr Armand Hammer and Alexander Schaffer (see Dealers and Experts). Advised by the Hammers and by Wartski's, she formed one of the finest collections of recent times, including three imperial Easter eggs (Plate 132, Cat. Plates 10, 12) and the celebrated lily-of-the-valley basket of 1896 (Plate 112). Her collection – today a foundation – is normally on view at the New Orleans Museum of Art.[42]

Malcolm Forbes of *The Forbes Magazine* owns the most important, and also most recent, collection of Fabergé in America today with over 130 items, including nine imperial Easter eggs (Plates 126, 137, 139, Cat. Plates 1, 2, 7, 15, 33, 51) and three other important eggs (Plates 142, 143, Cat. Plate 58). Many pieces came from Lansdell Christie,[43] an American whose collection, before it was put up for sale in 1967, comprised over one hundred choice items.

Two other major collections in America are that of Lillian T. Pratt, whose Fabergé pieces (left to the Virginia Museum of Fine Art, Richmond, in 1947[44]) include as many as five imperial Easter eggs (Plate 133, Cat. Plates 14, 32, 36, 52), and that of India Early Minshall in the Cleveland Museum of Art[45] that contains one imperial Easter egg (Cat. Plate 55).

One of Europe's most discerning collectors was the Swiss Maurice Sandoz, who owned some of Fabergé's finest works of art such as the Orange Tree Egg (Plate 139), before it was acquired by the Forbes Collection, and the Peacock Egg (Cat. Plate 25), as well as the Swan Egg (Plate 138) and the non-imperial Youssoupov Egg (Plate 140). King Farouk formed the largest collection of Fabergé objects in post-war times; it was dispersed in 1954 after his abdication. Other European collectors tend to be rather discreet about their collections. It is said that the Aga Khan, for instance, owns the most important menagerie of Fabergé animals in the world.

Dealers and Experts

Post-war collecting of Fabergé really began very soon following the master's death in 1920, when hundreds of refugees settled down in Paris. With the opening of 'A la Vieille Russie' by Jacques Zolotnitzky of Kiev in 1920, a centre was formed that attracted the Russian emigrés, who could thus find buyers when forced to dispose of their treasures. Zolotnitzky, who was joined in 1921 by his nephew, Léon Grinberg, soon had major pieces, including many Easter eggs, for sale.

1927 was a crucial date as far as the sales policy of the young Soviet state was concerned. Lenin, who had advocated the conservation of Russia's cultural heritage, had died in 1924. His successors relaxed the laws and began systematically to dispose of art objects from the imperial palaces in order to shore up the country's crumbling finances. The process got under way with the sale of part of the Russian crown jewels at Christie's in London. Simultaneously, overtures were made to Jacques Seligman one of the leading fine-art auctioneers in Paris with a view to securing his services as general agent for a projected series of further sales: however, he refused the offers.

In that very same year Emanuel Snowman of London, a partner in his father-in-law's shop in London, Wartski's, negotiated the acquisition of a 'gladstone bag full of imperial treasures' with an emissary of the Soviet state in Paris. Wartski's now became the European centre for acquiring Fabergé's work. Emanuel Snowman and his son, A. Kenneth Snowman, who is still considered perhaps the world's leading expert on the subject, have since catered to all the major English and European collectors.

Meanwhile, Dr Armand Hammer and his brothers had been trading with the Soviet Union since 1921, when they had obtained asbestos-mining rights and opened a pencil factory. When the Soviets decided to expropriate Hammer's factory, he was permitted to select from a large collection of objects, including many masterpieces by Fabergé—perhaps the very items shown to Seligman. Repaid in this manner, Hammer opened the Hammer Galleries of Russian Imperial Treasure in New York and began disposing his of acquisitions by means of a travelling exhibition, which ran from 1929 to 1935. At one point his collection numbered more than 2,000 items, including a series of the imperial Easter eggs. American enthusiasm was quickly aroused by the tragic connotations of these objects. The Hammer Collection was shown for the last time in 1933 at Lord & Taylors of New York. The great success of Fabergé among American collectors is partly due to this exceptional businessman and partly to Alexander Schaffer, who began as his assistant.

Alexander Schaffer opened his antique shop, also specializing in Russian works of art, in the Rockefeller Center in New York in the late 1920s. When the Soviet Union began to sell works of art, Schaffer started travelling regularly to Russia, where he acquired many important pieces by Fabergé, including a series of imperial Easter eggs (all those today in the Lillian T. Pratt Collection, see Collectors and Collections: 1917 until Today); he worked in tandem with Hammer. In 1941, when Zolotnitzky and Grinberg fled from Paris to New York because of the German occupation, Schaffer went into partnership with them and opened 'A la Vieille Russie', which is still the American centre for works of art by Fabergé.

Exhibitions

Western society and collectors really became aware of Fabergé in 1900, when his major works (the luxurious Easter eggs made for the Russian imperial family) were put on show in Paris at the World Fair. The first exhibition of Fabergé objects in England, organized by Lady Paget at a bazaar in the Albert Hall in 1904, was a great success, with Queen Alexandra buying a jade scent bottle and a diamond and enamel cigarette-holder. After 1906, Fabergé's works were on regular and discreet display in the London branch, which was visited by a continuous stream of customers, mostly from English Edwardian society but also including nearly all of the European nobility. Then came the First World War, the Russian Revolution and the closing of the House of Fabergé.

In 1927 Emanuel Snowman held an exhibition of all the imperial treasures he had purchased in Paris. Numerous articles appeared in the London press as proof of the interest aroused in the general public, and Fabergé's works were in the limelight once again. Similar exhibitions marked Snowman's return from Soviet Russia each year, whence he came laden with treasures and Easter eggs by Fabergé.

Lady Zia Wernher and her husband Lord Herbert organised a major showing of Russian art in 1935 at 1, Belgrave Square, the house of Madame Koch de Gooreynd; it included more than a hundred pieces by Fabergé, lent by all the great English Fabergé collectors including Her Majesty the Queen.[46]

Armand Hammer of New York, who had also returned from the Soviet Union laden with imperial treasure, began travelling all through the United States with his exhibition as early as 1929 (see Dealers and Experts).

In 1949, major public exhibitions were held by Wartski's and by 'A la Vieille Russie' (New York). Both were connected with the appearance of the first monograph on Fabergé, written by the ex-manager of Fabergé's London branch, H. C. Bainbridge. Wartski's showed nearly 400 pieces from all the main English collections, again including that of the king and queen,[47] while the New York exhibition comprised some 300 pieces from American collections, proving how much had already crossed the ocean by then.[48]

In 1953—the Coronation year—A. Kenneth Snowman published his monograph on Fabergé, and again an important exhibition was held at Wartski's, which met with both royal favour and popular success.[49]

The 1977 exhibition[50] held at the Victoria and Albert Museum on the occasion of Her Majesty the Queen's Silver Jubilee was organised by Kenneth Snowman and assembled some 520 pieces from all over the world. Given worldwide publicity by television and the press, the darkened rooms of the museum, lit by the glow of some of Fabergé's greatest masterpieces, became a place of pilgrimage for tens of thousands of visitors, many of whom queued for hours to get in.

Fabergé's Market and Prices

Before 1917

Despite what has been previously said on this subject, Fabergé's luxury objects were always relatively expensive. The fact that he rarely produced jewel-encrusted productions like his immediate predecessors and contemporaries probably made his art more accessible to the public. Nevertheless he was obliged to make certain concessions in this matter to his imperial or other rich patrons. Thus, among the more expensive standard pieces that were always available in his shops, Fabergé advertised diamond necklaces at prices of up to 50,000 roubles (£ 5,000./$ 24,000.). There is a record of a pearl *sautoir* or necklace made for Tsar Nicholas II as a present for Tsarina Alexandra that cost as much as 250,000 roubles (£ 25,000./$ 120,000.). The silver table-service in the gothic style ordered by Barbara Kelch, to replace one she did not like by Chlebnikov, cost 125,000 roubles (£ 12,500./$ 60,000.). These expensive commissions were, however, the exception, as were the imperial Easter eggs priced around 30,000 roubles (£ 3,000./$ 15,000.). [Exchange rates are those of the time.]

We now possess valuable information concerning the prices of the more current articles in Fabergé's shops. Quite recently the two sales ledgers in use in Fabergé's London branch (Plates 158–9) have been unearthed in a private collection. These volumes cover the period from 1907 to 1917 and provide information about cost prices of the articles in roubles and sales prices in pounds. The ratios between the two indicate that Fabergé's 'mark-up' averaged between ninety and a hundred percent.

It was possible to purchase a Fabergé article for as little as 5 roubles (10/-/$ 2.50): these were the popular miniature Easter eggs or pendants in enamel. More elaborate examples, however, cost up to 50 roubles (£ 5./$ 25.). Standard silver cigarette cases were also relatively cheap at an average of 100 roubles (£ 10./$ 50.), but more fancy cases—such as those made in blue and yellow enamel for Leopold Rothschild (Plate 152)—could cost as much as 800 roubles (£ 80./$ 400.). Clocks and frames were available at between 200 and 300 roubles (£ 20.–30./$ 100.–150.), although special commissions could cost as much as 1,000 roubles (£ 100./$ 500.). The little hardstone animal figures and Fabergé's lovely flowers (so popular with Queen Alexandra) were comparatively inexpensive, ranging from 180 roubles (£ 18./$ 90.) to about 600 roubles (£ 60./$ 300.).

We can attempt a brief comparison with other prices on the basis of figures given in the 1902 *Baedeker*. According to this source, hiring a fairly luxurious carriage and pair of horses in St. Petersburg cost between 10 and 15 roubles (£ 1–1/10-/$ 5–7) per day. Dinner at the famous Coubat Restaurant, only a few doors down the street from the House of Fabergé, is listed at 3 roubles (£6/-/$ 1.50)—wine extra. On the other hand the best seats at the Imperial Theatre, world-renowned for its performances of Russian opera and ballet, cost about 25 roubles (£ 2/10-/$ 12) on an ordinary night; at gala or charity performances they often cost many times that.

153–154   View of the front and lid of the so-called 'Youssoupov' Box, a musical automaton in enamelled gold, made in the Louis XVI style; the *en plein* panels are painted in *camaieu* (monochrome) sepia with views of the family castles: on the lid is Archangelskoie (near Moscow), celebrated for its picture gallery; on the front is the palace in St. Petersburg on the Moika Canal where Rasputin was murdered, 8.8 cm wide, signed, workmaster Henrik Wigström. This box was commissioned and presented as a silver-wedding present in 1907 by Princes Nicholas and Felix Youssoupov to their parents Felix and Zenaide Youssoupov. The crowned monograms of the family members appear on the cut corners of the box.

155   The Luton Hoo Freedom 'Box' is a nephrite cup mounted on two-coloured gold and standing on three ball feet; it has a double-headed eagle finial, 21.2 cm high, workmaster Michael Perchin. By family tradition this box was given to the Earl of Pembroke by Tsar Nicholas II when he was staying at Balmoral. (The Wernher Collection, Luton Hoo, Bedfordshire).

156   Hardstone figure of the gypsy Vara Panina. This is the most famous example of Fabergé's hardstone figures; it is composed of various types of jasper, a purpurine headdress and rose-diamond eyes, 17 cm high. Vara Panina was a gypsy singer, famous for her exceptional voice; she took poison and died on the stage of a Moscow restaurant while singing 'My Heart is Breaking' because of an unrequited love. This figure was last sold for Sfr. 200000.– (£ 26,000/$ 68,000). (A la Vieille Russie, New York).

153

154

1920–1949

Immediately following Fabergé's death, in the aftermath of the First World War, the name of Fabergé fell into temporary oblivion. In 1920 Jacques Zolotnitzky was able to purchase six large Easter eggs from Morgan of the Rue de la Paix for as little as 48,000 French francs (£925/$3,300.). In the upsurge of American interest in European art, these were disposed of only seven years later for 280,000 French francs (£2,240./$10,750.).

The first available Fabergé prices after the war are those from the sale of the Derek Berry Collection held at Christie's, London, in March 1934, when 87 objects were offered to the public. Prices were still very much in line with those paid at Fabergé's some 20 years previously. The top prices were for two imperial Easter eggs: £85 ($430.) for the first of Fabergé's eggs (Cat. Plate 1) and £110 ($560.) for the Resurrection Egg (Cat. Plate 2).

The reason for these low prices may be that a great deal of Fabergé's work was on the market through Wartski's at a time when only a few specialized collectors were interested. By 1934 Wartski's had already sold a number of imperial Easter eggs including the Orange Tree Egg (Plate 139) at £950 ($4,800.). Their sales ledgers also show how much of Fabergé's art was available at the time: a series of 100(!) hardstone animals was acquired in entirety from Popoff, Paris, for £1,100 ($5,600.).

It was, perhaps, the important 1935 Exhibition of Russian Art that changed the taste of buyers at auctions. In 1937 another sale took place at Christie's, with 183 objects by Fabergé, which sold for a total of about £4,200 ($20,500.); it included a number of items from Nicholas Fabergé's private collection. By this time prices had definitely began to go up. Further sales in 1947 and 1949—the Eckstein and Gordon Bois collections—at Sotheby's underlined this trend.

1954–1965

After the Second World War came that memorable sale of the King Farouk Collection by the Egyptian Government in 1954. In 65 lots some 150 objects by Fabergé were knocked down for a total of about 35,000 Egyptian pounds (£32,000./$85,000.). Several pieces originally sold by Christie's or Sotheby's before the war came up for sale again. With only a few exceptions, all the objects acquired by or for the King in the ten preceding years had doubled or tripled their value. The top prices in this sale were fetched by the small Easter egg (Cat. Plate 58) made for Barbara Kelch (E£4,200/£3,800/$10,000) and the Swan egg (Plate 138) of 1906 (E£6,400/£5,800/$16,000).

Only five years later, when Christie's sold the collection of Sir Charles Dodds, prices for minor objects were seen to be rising more rapidly still, flowers fetching £900 ($2,500), and animal carvings being sold for over £1,500 ($4,200). The famous purpurine cat, which had been sold by Wartski's in the late 1920s for £75 ($360) now fetched £1,732 ($4,800). The next time it came up for sale—in Geneva—the price was SFr70,000 (£10,600/$24,000).

157 The Cuckoo-Clock Egg, presented by Tsar Nicholas II either to his mother, Marie Feodorovna, or to his wife, Alexandra Feodorovna, in 1900. It is made of varicoloured gold with violet enamel over a moiré guilloché pattern with white opaque enamel, diamonds and pearls. This egg contains a singing-bird automaton, 20.3 cm high, signed and dated 1900, workmaster Michael Perchin, 1899–1908. When a button is pressed, a circular grille surmounting the egg opens, and a cuckoo with naturalistic feathers and ruby eyes appears and starts to sing, moving its beak and wings. This egg was last sold for Sfr. 620000.– (£80,000/$190,000). (Bernard Solomon Collection, Los Angeles).

The first milestone in the history of modern Fabergé prices is the sale of the Lansdell Christie Collection at Parke-Bernet, New York, in 1967, where 66 lots topped the $300,000 (£107,000) mark. The tendency visible in the Farouk sale was further accentuated: compared to cost prices in the London auction rooms only five years previously, values again doubled. In this sale, record prices were obtained for a piece of miniature furniture ($39,000/£13,400) and for a diamond-set imperial presentation box ($40,000/£13,800).

The latest series of major sales began in 1973–4 at Christie's in Geneva, where specialist Russian auctions were soon a regular feature. In these years Fabergé prices reached an all-time high. Here the 'Balletta' box (Plate 150), which had fetched $30,000 (£10,700) at the Lansdell Christie sale, now cost as much as SFr190,000 (£24,700/$61,000); a hardstone figure, Vara Panina (Plate 156), of a type that had been fetching £7,000 ($20,000) around 1960, now sold for SFr200,000 (£26,000/$68,000). SFr360,000 (£54,000/$125,000) were paid by a Persian collector for the tray (Plate 145) presented by the Dutch Colony to Queen Wilhelmina of the Netherlands in 1901, while the imperial Cuckoo egg of 1900 (Plate 157) went to an American buyer for the world-record price of SFr620,000 (£80,000/$190,000).

Since then no major items have been available at sales, but small objects are still rising rapidly in value. In the Robert Strauss sale held by Christie's in London in 1976, 59 lots sold for £304,860 ($570,000), with flowers as high as £17,000 ($32,000) for a lily-of-the-valley spray (Plate 110) and £24,000 ($45,000) for a spray of gentian.

Good Fabergé work always was—and still is—very much a collector's item for a rich man. Owing to its scarcity, prices have been soaring continuously. Any major article by this artist will always command an exceptional price. Provenance has, however, become a vital consideration as fakes begin to inundate the market.

158–159 Two pages from the 1912 sales ledger of Fabergé's London branch: In Pl. 158 the dormouse in Pl. 107 (Collection of Her Majesty the Queen) is entered under 5 November as sold to Queen Alexandra of England. The page in Pl. 159 documents a visit to Fabergé's, on Christmas Eve 1912, by Queen Alexandra and her sister Marie Feodorovna. (The Fabergé family archives.)

160–163 Imitations of Fabergé articles:
160 An ashtray of enamelled gold by Stiquel, Paris, c. 1925.
161 A modern copy of the Coronation Coach Egg; compare with Pl. 126.
162 Forget-me-nots in gold and turquoise with crudely cut nephrite leaves, in a rock-crystal vase, stamped with the Fabergé mark used in Paris.
163 A modern copy of the Serpent Clock Egg of particularly bad quality; compare with Pl. 6 of the catalogue of Fabergé's Easter eggs.

164–165 Examples of technical details: *(left)* chased borders with precisely chased foliage by Fabergé (a) and by a contemporary imitator (b); *(right)* hinges of cigarette cases with hinges hardly visible by Fabergé (a) and by a contemporary imitator (b).

166 Comparison of firm marks on the lining of a genuine fitted case *(above)* and a fake one *(below)*. The genuine mark is more precise. Fabergé's maple-wood cases are works of art in themselves (see Pl. 167); fakers often cut the corners of their cases, while the corners of Fabergé's cases are carefully rounded.

167 A selection of Fabergé's cases made of wood, felt and leather. The wooden boxes, hitherto thought to be of holly-wood, are actually of sycamore-maple. We are grateful to Mrs Plu of the Laboratoire d'Ethnobotanique of the Musée national d'histoire naturelle, Paris, for this information. (The Forbes Collection, New York).

168–169 Examples of fake signatures with badly struck marks, obliterating older marks and differing from the genuine punches in the lettering.

Date.	Customer's Name.	Description of Goods.	Stock Number.	Selling Price Details £ s. d.	Total £ s. d.	S.L. Folio.	Cost Price Rbls. Cop.
Nov		B/forward			1,034.16..		6,308.40
5	Queen Alexandra	Dormouse, agate, gold straws, 2 cab. sapphs:	22631	33 - -			181.
		Elephant, neph: 2 roses	22633	11 15 -			54.
		Frame, jadeite, rasp. en:	22396	18 - -			74.
		Bonbon, powpowrine, white opg. & green opl. enl.	22449	23 15 -			117.
		Pendant, 1 blue mecca 1 brill & diads. plat. chain	9487?	30 - -	116 10 -	1	181.
1	R. Woods Bliss	Cig'th holder case, lilac enal. gold mounts 72°	22494		8 - -	21	33.
1	Pcc. Alex. of Battenberg	Ring, 1 sapp: cab. 4 4th cts.	9067?		160 - -	388	955
8	Ino. E. Yates	Bowl, large, nephrite, on neph. pedestal, supported by 3 sil: dolphins	18783	nett	200 - -	20	1,000 -
1	D. Mc Calmont	Cig'th case, mauve enal.	22430		23 - -	19	136
1	Mrs Collbran	Koosh, green oak, silver	8143?06	8 15 -			49.
		Gumbottle, lilac enal.	22773	10 10 -	19 5 -	35?	65.
1	Baron A. de Goldschmidt-Rothschild	Papercutter, tort'shell, steel blue en: & diad. rim	22698	39 - -			228.
		Matchstand, jadeite, rim in gold with green enl 4 cal supps & diads	22472	28 - -	67 - -	213	139
		C/forward			£ 1,628·11·0		R. 9,520.40

Date	Customer's Name	Description of Goods	Stock Number	Selling Price Details £ s. d.	Selling Price Total £ s. d.	S. L. Folio	Cost Price Rbls. Cop.
1912							
Dec		Brought forward			£ 1,851 14 "		10,420.99
24	Wⁿ Koch	Brooch, 1 star sap: & roses	91195	10 10 "			55 .
		Pendant, mecca, wht. enl.	93620	10 " "			53 .
		Frame, wht. maple; silvᵉˢ	21310	5 15 "			31 .
		Tiepin, chryso & red enl.	94141	4 10 "	30 15 "	336	22 .
	Queen Alexandra	Bracelet, sil. 2 moons, roses	95221	15 " "			75
		Do platinum; gold	9670	12 10 "			78 .
		Fan, lt. blue en: gold mts.					
		4 ornts. rubies; white opl. e	17524	26 " "			118 .
		Links, 4 blue meccas, plat.	95199	14 " "			80 .
		Elephant, powpoweine	22623	11 15 "	79 5 "	1	55 .
1	Dow. Empress	Pendant, 1 ameth: diads	91102	27 " "			141
	Marie of Russia	Pencil & cutter, blue enl.	21774	5 5 "			31
		Locket, st. blue enl. 1 brll.	95826	8 15 "	41 " "	6	49
1	Mⁿˢ Cole	Tiepin, gold 56; 1 neph:					
	(Sandringham.)	cab. white opq. enamel	#10838	gratis	" "	1	22 "
26	G. Duke Michael	Neck ornt. brlls & roses					
		mtd. on black silk rib:	S. H.	nett	120 " "	366	855 .
1	King Manuel	Cig. case, oval, lt. pink enl.	22842		22 " "	375	1121 "
27	A. J. Nagliano	Links, gold, 4 sap. cab. brlls	91791	36 10 "			185 .
		Do , 4 sap cab; diads.	73708	57 " "			335 .
		Buttons, (4) wht. opl. enl.					
		& roses (part of set)	95832	8 8 "	101 18 "	39	46 .
		Carried forward			£ 2246 12 "		R. 12,772.99

164 a   b

165 a   b

166

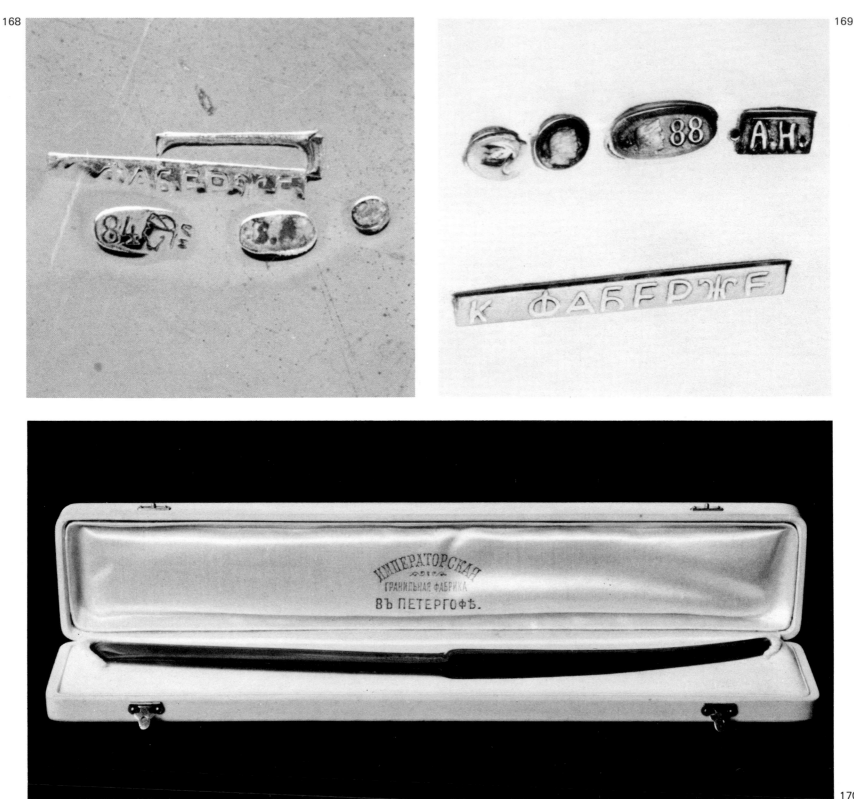

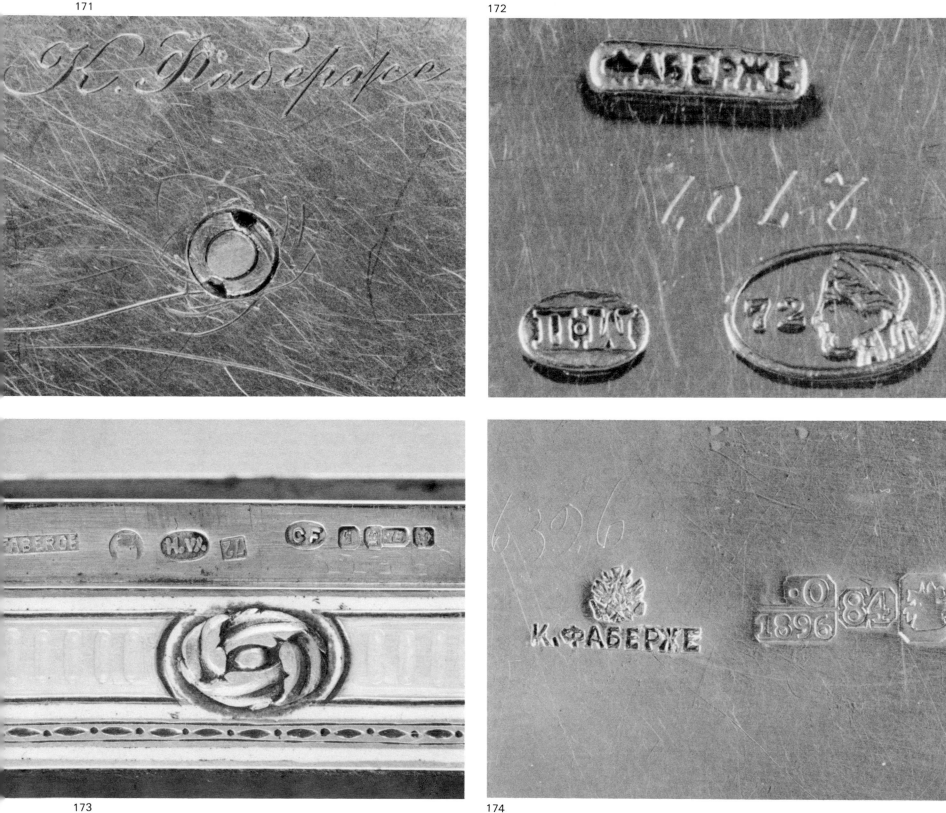

ФАБЕРЖЕ
С.ПЕТЕРБУРГЪ
МОСКВА, ОДЕССА
КІЕВЪ, ЛОНДОНЪ

Fabergé and Fake Fabergé

170 A paperknife of nephrite in a maple-wood case inscribed "Imperial hardstone manufacture in Peterhof". The similarity of both the object and the case to Fabergé's production would lead one to believe that the imperial manufacturers also worked for Fabergé, especially in late years when snowballing commissions could no longer be dealt with by Fabergé's Ekatarinsky Canal workshops.

171–174 Examples of genuine Fabergé signatures:

171 Engraved signature on the heart-shaped frame in Pls. 21–22.

172 Signature on the sedan-chair in Pls. 89–90; the rare *kokoshnik* mark with the initials of the assay-master Jakov Ljapunov, the initials of workmaster Michael Perchin and a scratched Fabergé inventory number, 2707.

173 Marks on a gold-mounted case of nephrite (not illustrated) made for the London market: signature in Roman letters, a circular *kokoshnik* mark, the initials of workmaster Henrik Wigström, a *zolotnik* mark 72, the Roman initials of Fabergé, an English control mark for imported gold wares with the letter-date for 1911 and Fabergé's inventory number, 22338.

174 Marks on the silver-gilt cream jug in Pl. 36: imperial warrant mark of Moscow with the initials L.O. of an unidentified assay-master, the date 1896 and Fabergé's inventory number, 6326.

175 Stamp on the lining of the cover of one of Fabergé's maple-wood cases (all his objects were sold in such cases): double-headed eagle, the name of Fabergé in Cyrillic characters and the names of the cities where Fabergé was represented —St. Petersburg, Moscow (after 1887), Odessa (after 1890), Kiev (after 1905), London (after 1906). Cases with 'Petrograd' instead of 'St. Petersburg' date from after the outbreak of the First World War. Some rare cases are stamped 'Nishegorodskaya Jamarka' for the Nishnj Novgorod Fair where Fabergé occasionally exhibited his goods.

Fabergé was the inspirator, the constant source of new ideas for a number of first-class craftsmen working on his behalf. These were not only active within his own workshops but also in other firms both in St. Petersburg and Moscow as well as in other countries. It has been said that some hardstone animals sold by Fabergé were in fact carved outside Fabergé's own workshops. This might possibly explain why two main styles prevail in Fabergé's animal world: the naturalistic, highly finished carvings originating from the workshop on the Obvodny Canal, and the more stylized statuettes of lesser quality possibly from elsewhere. Fabergé also had a working connection with Cartier's of Paris whence, at a certain stage, came the rock-crystal vases for his flower arrangements.

Most of Fabergé's cloisonné enamel objects were commissioned outside his Moscow workshops. Articles made for him by Fedor Rückert (his main source) always bear Fabergé's imperial warrant mark overstriking Rückert's punch. This cannot always be said of items provided by the firms of Saltykov, of Maria Semenova or of those by the *Artels*, which Fabergé retailed. These can often only be recognized by Fabergé's original maple-wood cases.

It has become very difficult to know where to draw the line between what can safely be regarded as Fabergé, and what not, especially in view of the fact that Fabergé even acquired objects of art on his travels, which were available for sale at his shops alongside his own products in the same maple-wood cases; therefore, it is no longer sufficient evidence of authorship to know that an object was bought at Fabergé's.

After Fabergé's death and the closing down of all the workshops, a number of craftsmen and workmasters emigrated and continued to work in the West. Johan Victor Aarne is known to be one of these, as well as Albert Holmström (August's adopted son) and of Oskar Pihl, Jr. A workshop in Helsinki produced a large number of hardstone animals often mistaken for originals. The most important expatriate workshop was active in Paris under Eugène Fabergé and Andrea Marchetti. Many pieces amongst the large number of objects circulating in Paris after 1924 are said to have been repaired by Eugène; others were embellished with precious stones, modified, or even made anew. Some quite stunning pieces from Fabergé's in Paris are said to stand unrecognized in many a major collection today. Also working in Paris were Silvio Marucelli and Stiquel, both fine craftsmen who changed the original aspect of a number of pieces and made objects in the style of Fabergé; there was also a workshop producing large numbers of hardstone animals.

After the first public exhibitions of Fabergé's work in both Europe and America (1933, 1935, 1937 and 1949) and after the pioneering books of Bainbridge (1949) and Snowman (1953), the owning of *objets de fantasie* by this great artist became fashionable among the rich. Numerous copies were produced in Idar-Oberstein, Germany, with no intent of deceiving. Fraudulent jewellers later added Fabergé marks and sold them as genuine. Since only a limited number of pieces were available at the time and the demand grew rapidly, fakes and forgeries of all kinds inundated the market. Dozens of 'Fabergé' flowers were in fact Cartier productions. Imitations of his flowers in the art-deco style can still be seen today in major private collections.

From the mid-1960s, fake Fabergé also started appearing from the Soviet Union (fake marks: Plates 168–9). Many objects left the country through diplomatic channels or through emigrés. Tourists acquired the strangest objects, all bearing Fabergé marks. It has only recently become known in the West that a certain forger was apparently sentenced to six years forced labour for faking Fabergé's art. It is said that much of what has left the Soviet Union in the last 15 years is the work of this man; his main speciality was hardstone figures, some of which seem to have passed the test of various auctions in America. Another easy means of leading buyers astray (and apparently used by him) was the re-marking of cloisonné enamels by Semenova, Saltykov and others, adding Fabergé's punch and thus doubling their value. Many of these pieces are today in the hands of Western diplomats.

Since about 1970, faking Fabergé has become a favourite occupation of many first-class craftsmen, who are becoming more and more enterprising. Very many objects by contemporary Russian artists such as Sumin, Britzin and Denisov-Ouralsky are frequently re-marked. These objects, at least, are old and have their own intrinsic value.

Lately even copies of Fabergé's imperial Easter eggs of very low technical standard (Plate 161) are being produced in a Latin American country and sold to unsuspecting tourists for prices around the $25,000 region. These, however, are virtually worthless.

Three categories of fakes can be said conclusively to exist:

a) Objects embellished, through re-enamelling, re-gilding, re-decoration with precious stones or re-marking with lacking punches. (These objects are genuine, but their value has been enhanced by later additions. It is virtually impossible to identify this type of falsification.)

b) Genuine objects made by Russian contemporaries of Fabergé who imitated him (e.g. Hahn, Köchli, Sumin, Britzin) and that have been turned into Fabergés by subsequent marking (Plates 168–9). (It is indeed very difficult for any imitator to resist the great increase in value of these objects occasioned by employing this simple means. Numerous pieces first appear on the market with a competitor's punch and later return with Fabergé's mark. Only the practiced eye of an expert can recognize these imitations. Difference in style and quality makes it possible to identify the genuine article, but to recognize fake punches needs years of practice.)

c) Complete forgeries, almost without exception bearing the Fabergé signature; some might well have been produced before the Second World War, the greater part, however, appeared after publication of Snowman's book, from 1953 onwards. (These forgeries, in most cases, are direct copies of originals which, as a rule, have only been made once. For this reason all duplicates should always be considered with caution, see Plates 160–3.)

The forger's most difficult problem is to imitate Fabergé's technical perfection: no enamel today can compete with that of Fabergé. The guilloché enamel, the hinges and the chasing of fake objects always leave something to be desired (Plates 164–5). But even here it must be admitted that some of the contemporary forgers reach such perfection, that Fabergé himself might well have accepted them in his workshop!

Hallmarks and Signatures on Fabergé's Objects

The Standard Marks

The Russian gold and silver standards in general use at this time where reckoned in *zolotniks*. Ninety-six *zolotniks* correspond to pure silver and to 24-carat gold. The most frequently found proportions for silver are 84 and 88 *zolotniks*: the rarer 91-*zolotnik* marks often help to identify objects made for export. The corresponding standards in the West are 875, 916 and 947/1000, while English 'sterling' silver presupposes a standard of at least 925/1000. For gold the Russian standard marks are 56 and 72 *zolotniks*, corresponding to 14- and 18-carat gold. Fabergé mainly used the higher standards of these metal alloys.

The Russian State Marks

Nineteenth Century (until 1899):

The following marks are found on objects, together with the assay-master's initials and the date:

1      For St. Petersburg: the arms of the city, the crossed anchors and vertical sceptre

2

3   For Moscow: the arms of the city, St. George and the Dragon.

1899–1908

Kokoshnik mark, facing left. This mark shows the head of a girl in profile, wearing the traditional Russian high headdress called *kokoshnik*. The origin of each piece can be recognized by the assay-master's initials behind the head.

4      For St. Petersburg: the Cyrillic initials Ja. L. for Jakov Ljapunov

5   or A. R. for A. Richter.

6   For Moscow: the Cyrillic initials I. L. for Ivan Lebedkin.

The oval *kokoshnik* mark may be replaced by the silver standard-mark, occasionally giving the assay-master's initials.

Kokoshnik mark facing right. The head and initials no longer seem engraved but appear in relief. The origin of each piece can be recognized by a Greek letter within the mark:

For St. Petersburg: the Greek letter alpha.

 7

For Moscow: the Greek letter delta (Odessa: Greek k; Kiev: Greek n).

8

A small, circular *kokoshnik* mark is found on objects weighing less than 8.5 grams (2 *zolotniks*) or on separate parts.

9

Fabergé's Signatures

St. Petersburg

Fabergé's full signature (without initial) in Cyrillic characters, wherever possible;

ФАБЕРЖЕ 10

Fabergé's initials in Cyrillic characters for small objects.

КФ 11

Numerous pieces made in St. Petersburg do not carry Fabergé's signature. All, however, are marked with the initials of the workmaster responsible for the article. Pieces made by Fabergé's brother Agathon (1862–95) may be signed A. Fabergé in Cyrillic characters.

Moscow

К.ФАБЕРЖЕ 12

Articles made in the Moscow workshop are marked K. Fabergé in Cyrillic characters together with the double-headed eagle as proof of the imperial warrant granted by Tsar Alexander III in 1884. In contrast to St. Petersburg practice, the Moscow workmaster did not sign the articles he produced.

К.ФАБЕРЖЕ 13

Exception: Fabergé's imperial warrant mark (the double-headed eagle) often in a separate punch and the signature with or without the first initial K appear exceptionally on silver articles made for or sold by the St. Petersburg workshop. This mark can only be found in conjunction with silver objects made by Nevalainen, Rappoport, Wäkewä, the unidentified I. W. and the First Silver *Artel* (I. C. A.), who apparently worked for both workshops.

КФАБЕРЖЕ 14

Articles for Export

15  Articles made for export for the London branch, are marked with Fabergé's name in Roman letters and/or with the Roman initials C. F., invariably together with English import-marks.

16 **CF**

All objects should carry an inventory number—as is visible on plate 173 next to Fabergé's signature, as well as on plates 172 and 174. Only the smallest items, such as the miniature Easter eggs, were not identified in this manner.

The Workmasters

17 **ВА** Johan VICTOR AARNE (1863–after 1920) born in Finland, workmaster for Fabergé from 1891. His signature is to be found on enamelled gold and silver articles. Aarne left Fabergé before 1917 and opened his own workshop in Viipuri, Finland, where he remained active until the early 1920s; his signature there was J. V. A.

18 **ФА** FEDOR AFANASSIEV made small articles of high quality in enamel (miniature Easter eggs), small frames and cigarette cases.

19 **ЯА** Karl Gustav HJALMAR ARMFELDT, born in Hangö, Finland, workmaster from 1895. He worked for Fabergé until 1916, producing enamelled objects.

20 **АГ** ANDREJ GORIANOV took over from Reimer after his death in 1898 and also specialized in cigarette cases.

21 **A+H** AUGUST Frederik HOLLMING (1854–1915) born in Loppis, Finland; apprentice 1876, workmaster 1880. Specialist for all types of case, but mainly less elaborate gold and silver cigarette cases or simple enamel boxes. Occasionally he produced small enamelled jewels.

22 **АН** AUGUST Wilhelm HOLMSTRÖM (1829–1903) born in Helsingfors, Finland; master in 1857 with his own workshop. Senior member of Fabergé's workshop, he was head jeweller and also produced parts for composite articles. His son ALBERT HOLMSTRÖM (1876–1925), also a jeweller, continued in his father's footsteps after his death and used the same mark.

23 **ЕК** ERIK August KOLLIN (1836–1901), of Finnish origin; workmaster 1868. Originally worked for Holmström. Head workmaster in 1870, when he opened his own workshop, producing exclusively for Fabergé. Head workmaster until 1886. Specialized in gold and silver articles, most of them in an archaic style typical of the period.

24 **ГЛ** G. LUNDELL was head workmaster in Odessa.

25 **АМ** ANDERS MICHELSON (born in 1839 in Finland) made gold cigarette cases and small enamelled objects.

26 **A.N** ANDERS Johan NEVALAINEN (born 1858 in Pielisjärvi, Finland) apprentice in St. Petersburg in 1876; workmaster for Fabergé in 1885. He made smaller silver and gold objects, enamelled frames and cigarette cases in gold or silver.

27 **GN** GABRIEL NIUKKANEN had an independent workshop in the Kazanskaya Street in 1898. He made plain gold cigarette cases, which only exceptionally bore Fabergé's signature.

28 **M.П** MICHAEL Evlampievitch PERCHIN (1860–1903), of Russian peasant extraction, succeeded Kollin in 1886 as head workmaster. His workshop produced all types of *objets*

de fantaisie in gold, enamel and hardstones, mostly baroque or rococo in style, all of the highest aesthetic and technical standards.

OSKAR Woldemar PIHL, son of Knut Oskar Pihl and of the daughter of August Holmström; workmaster in Holmström's workshop, he made small items of jewellery such as tie pins, some of which are enamelled.

JULIUS Alexandrovitch RAPPOPORT (1864–1916) had his own workshop at Ekatarininski Canal from 1883, which he retained when Fabergé moved his workmaster staff to the house in Bolshaya Morskaya Street. Rappoport was head silversmith and produced large objects and services, as well as silver animals.

WILHELM REIMER (born in Pernau, Lettland, died c. 1898) made small enamel and gold objects.

Philip THEODOR RINGE had his own workshop from 1893 and made objects in enamelled gold or silver.

FEDOR RÜCKERT, born in Moscow, of German origin, made articles in cloisonné enamel in Moscow. Fabergé's Moscow signature often obliterates Rückert's initials. Rückert also sold his cloisonné objects independently, which explains why a number of his pieces bear no Fabergé signature.

EDUARD Wilhelm SCHRAMM, born in St. Petersburg, of German origin, worked for Fabergé before 1899 making cigarette cases and gold objects; in most cases he signed only with his own initials.

VLADIMIR SOLOVIEV took over Ringe's workshop after his death, making similar objects. His initials can often be found under the enamel on pieces made for export to England.

ALFRED THIELEMANN (date of birth unknown, died between 1890 and 1910), of German origin; master from 1858 and active as jeweller for Fabergé from 1880. Thielemann produced trinkets and small pieces of jewellery; his place was taken after his death by his son Karl Rudolph Thielemann.

The same mark AT was also used by three other masters who did not work for Fabergé: Alexander Tillander produced objects in the style of Fabergé for the firm of Hahn; A. Tobinkov was a workmaster in the firm of silversmiths, Nichols & Plincke; the third was A. Treiden.

STEPHAN WÄKEVÄ (born 1833 in Finland), workmaster from 1856, made articles of silver or silver mounts. Was followed after his death by his son Alexander Wäkevä, whose signature AW can be found on a number of Fabergé's silver pieces.

Henrik WIGSTRÖM (1862– c. 1930), of Finnish origin, Perchin's assistant from 1886 and head workmaster after his death in 1903. His objects are often similar to those of Perchin but tend to be in the Louis XVI or Empire style. Nearly all the hardstone animals and figures were produced under his supervision.

First Silver-*Artel* (1. Serebriannaya Artel.) The *Artels* were cooperatives of jewellers, gold and silversmiths working independently. They first appeared in Moscow about 1896 and are classified by numbers. Thirty Moscow *Artels* are known at present. The Silver-*Artel* was active in St. Petersburg between 1908 and 1917, making large silver articles and also a number of objects in guilloché enamel. Fabergé commissioned silver items from the first Silver-*Artel* and retailed articles from the third *Artel*.

Marks of workmasters whose signatures appear in conjunction with Fabergé's mark but who have not been identified:

M·П — 29
OP — 30
I.P. — 31
W.R — 32
T.R — 33
Ф.P. — 34
ES — 35
BC — 36
AT — 37
S·W — 38
A.W — 39
H.W. — 40
ICA — 41
З·я·А — 42
AR J.W. 43/44/45

Notes

1 The major part of the Fabergé family's and firm's history is based on the monographs and articles of H.C. Bainbridge (Biblio. no. 1) and A.K. Snowman (Biblio. no. 2). Further information derives from unpublished notes made by L. Grinberg, based on conversations with Eugène and Alexander Fabergé and remaining members of the Fabergé family.

2 For contemporary assessment of the exhibited pieces, see Chanteclair (Biblio. no. 16), pp. 61 ff.

3 Bainbridge (Biblio. no. 13), p. 306.

4 Snowman (Biblio. no. 20), pp. 139 ff.

5 This is further documented by Fabergé's London sales ledgers, where returns of objects not wanted may be found entered at the end of each month's accounts.

6 See M.A. Nekrasova, *The Wars of Liberation 1812 and Russian Art* (in Russian), Moscow, 1969, p. 67.

7 Chanteclair (Biblio. no. 16), pp. 66 and 68.

8 E. Schwedeler-Meyer, 'Goldsmithwork' in *The Crisis of the Applied Arts,* (in German, R. Gaul, ed.) Leipzig, 1901, p. 132.

9 Fabergé's private collections were taken over by the Hermitage Museum after 1917; cf. V. Mavrodin, *Fine Arms from Tula,* The Hermitage, Leningrad, 1977, p. 5.

10 See K. Butler, *Meissen Porcelain Figures of the 18th Century,* (in Russian), Leningrad, 1977, where 15 animals with the provenance 'Collection of A.K. Fabergé' are illustrated, pp. 338 ff.

11 See *Les Années '25': Collections du Musée des Arts Décoratifs,* catalogue, (Y. Brunhammer, ed.), Paris, 1966, p. 136.

12 Berniakovitch (Biblio. no. 15), pp. 81 and 83.

13 According to Eugène Fabergé and quoted by L. Grinberg (unpublished manuscript); see also Snowman (Biblio. no. 2), p. 120.

14 Schwedeler-Meyer, *op. cit.* p. 130.

15 C. Truman, 'The Master of the Easter Egg' in *Apollo,* CVI, no. 185 (July, 1977), p. 72.

16 See L. Giesz, *Phänomenologie des Kitsches* (in German) 2nd ed., Munich, 1971, for basic information about the *kitsch* problem.

17 See Roy Strong, foreword of the catalogue (Biblio. no. 39), where he speaks of a 'dismissive regard toward *objets de luxe.*'

18 Bainbridge (Biblio. no. 1), p. 147.

19 'La rareté du platine' in *Revue de la bijouterie, joaillerie et orfèvrerie,* no. 36 (April, 1903), p. 419.

20 Snowman (Biblio. no. 2), illustration 78, from the Robert Strauss Collection (Christie's, London, 9 March 1976, lot 12).

21 See Houillon (Biblio. no. 19), p. 98.

22 Snowman (Biblio. no. 2), pl. III, illustrates one of Fabergé's original enamel charts with 144 enamel colours and guilloché patterns.

23 See A.E. Fersman, *Les Joyaux du Trésor de Russie,* Moscow, 1925/26, where A. Faberger *(sic)* is mentioned as jewellery expert.

24 McNab Dennis (Biblio. no. 21), p. 236.

25 *Stolitsa i Usadba* (Biblio. no. 24), p. 14.

26 Catalogue: Christie, Manson & Woods, 6 May, 1938, lot 133.

27 Snowman (Biblio. no. 2), pls. 309–10.

28 Snowman (Biblio. no. 2), pls. 307–8.

29 Snowman (Biblio. no. 2), pl. 342.

30 Snowman (Biblio. no. 2), pls. 311–12.

31 H. Waterfield and C. Forbes (Biblio. no. 12), pl. 39.

32 Christie's (International) S.A., Geneva, 27 April, 1977, lot 481, where it was sold for S Fr. 550,000 (£ 120,000/$ 220,000).

33 Snowman (Biblio. no. 2), pl. 387.

34 Snowman (Biblio. no. 2), pls. 334–5.

35 Snowman (Biblio. no. 2), pl. 337.

36 Christie's (International) S.A., Geneva, 16 November 1978, lots 615–23.

37 Ross (Biblio. no. 9), pls. 108 ff.

38 Ross (Biblio. no. 9), pl. 57.

39 Bainbridge (Biblio. no. 1), pl. 87.

40 A selection of objects from this collection were sold at Christie's (International) S.A., Geneva, on 26 April, 1978: lots 287–305, 336, 363, 379.

41 Ross (Biblio. no. 9).

42 Grady and Fagaly (Biblio. no. 4).

43 Waterfield and Forbes (Biblio. no. 12).

44 Lesley (Biblio. no. 6).

45 Hawley (Biblio. no. 5).

46 Bibliography no. 27.

47 Bibliography no. 29.

48 Bibliography no. 30.

49 Bibliography no. 32.

50 Bibliography no. 38.

Glossary of Technical Terms

art nouveau: a style prevailing in Europe *c.* 1890–1917, with decorative motifs based on plant forms

baroque: a florid style prevalent in Europe in the 17th and 18th centuries

bonbonnière: a small recipient for sweetmeats

bowenite: Russian jade of a pale milky green colour

bratina: a Russian punch bowl

brilliant-cut diamond: a circular-cut diamond with a flat top

burrwood: wood of the banyan tree

cabochon: a precious stone domed and polished but not faceted

camaieu sepia: monochrome painting in lilac

chasing: engraving or embossing done by hand

champlevé enamel: enamel melted into compartments excavated in a metal object

cloisonné enamel: enamel melted into compartments formed by thin plates applied on a flat surface

dendritic: tree-like

Empire style: a style prevailing in Europe under Napoleon's rule, *c.* 1804–15

engine-turned: engraved by machine with a regular pattern

en plein enamel: fully enamelled or painted-on enamel

finial: crowning ornament of a cover

fluted: cut with wide parallel stripes

gadroon(ed): (decorated with) a set of convex curves forming a continuous pattern

grisaille: monochrome painting in grey

guilloché enamel: translucent enamel over an engine-turned *(q.v.)* decoration

historicism: a style inspired by previous styles and prevailing in the 19th century

kovsh: a traditional Russian drinking vessel, shaped as a bird; later an object of presentation for services to the crown

Mecca stone: cabochon *(q.v.)* chalcedony that is stained pink

moiré: having a watered, clouded appearance

niello: a metallic alloy for filling in engraved designs on silver or metal

obsidian: dark and coloured vitreous volcanic rock

palisander: Brazilian rosewood

parcel-gilt: partly gilded

pendant: a loose, hanging ornament or jewel

plique-à-jour enamel: transparent enamel that is melted into compartments that are not backed

reeded: cut with thin parallel stripes

rocaille: a scroll or spiral ornament typical of the rococo *(q.v.)* period

rococo: the German equivalent of the Louis XV style, characterized by scroll or rocaille *(q.v.)* decoration

rock-crystal: transparent quartz

rose(-cut) diamond: a diamond with the top cut into triangular facets

samorodok: a Russian decoration simulating natural nugget gold

scarab: an Egyptian beetle

Scherzbecher: a drinking vessel comprising some sort of device to play a prank usually causing the drinker to get wet

swag: garlands of flowers or foliage

table-cut (portrait) diamond: a thin diamond, cut with flat top surface and shaped as a table

tcharka: small, usually round, Russian drinking cup for vodka

Catalogue of Fabergé's Easter Eggs

Presented by Tsar Alexander III to his wife, Marie Feodorovna:

1 The First Hen Egg. Probable date 1884, unmarked (The Forbes Collection, New York)

2 The Resurrection Egg. Probable date 1885/6. Workmaster M. Perchin (The Forbes Collection, New York)

3 Blue Enamel Ribbed Egg. Probably presented to Tsarina Marie Feodorovna. Possible date 1886/7. Workmaster M. Perchin (Stavros Niarchos Collection, Paris)

5 The Danish Silver Jubilee Egg. Said to have been dated 1888. Lost (See also Pl. 122)

6 The Serpent Clock Egg. Probably presented to Tsarina Marie Feodorovna. Possible date 1889. Workmaster M. Perchin (private collection, Switzerland)

7 The Spring Flowers Egg. Probably presented to Tsarina Marie Feodorovna. Possible date 1890. Workmaster M. Perchin (The Forbes Collection, New York)

8 The Azova Egg. Probable date 1891. Workmaster M. Perchin (Armoury Museum, the Kremlin, Moscow)

9 The Twelve-monogram Egg (The Silver Anniversary Egg). Probable date 1892. Workmaster M. Perchin (M.M. Post Collection: the Hillwood Collection, Washington, D.C.)

10 The Caucasus Egg. Dated 1893. Workmaster M. Perchin (M.G. Gray Foundation Collection, New Orleans)

11 The Renaissance Egg. Dated 1894. Workmaster M. Perchin (The Forbes Collection, New York) (See also Pl. 137)

Presented by Tsar Nicholas II to his mother, Marie Feodorovna:

12 The Danish Palace Egg. Probable date 1895. Workmaster M. Perchin (M.G. Gray Foundation Collection, New Orleans)

14 The Pelican Egg. Dated 1897. Workmaster M. Perchin (L.T. Pratt Collection: Virginia Museum of Fine Arts, Richmond)

15 The Lilies-of-the-valley Egg. Dated 1898. Workmaster M. Perchin (The Forbes Collection, New York)

16 The Pansy Egg. Dated 1899. Workmaster M. Perchin (private collection, U.S.A.)

17 The Cuckoo-clock Egg. Dated 1900. Workmaster M. Perchin (Bernard Solomon Collection, Los Angeles) (See also Pl. 157)

19 The Gatchina Palace Egg. Probable date 1902. Workmaster M. Perchin (The Walters Art Gallery, Baltimore) (See also Pl. 131)

21 The Alexander III Commemorative Egg. Dated 1904. (Armoury Museum, the Kremlin, Moscow)

25 The Peacock Egg. Dated 1908. Workmaster H. Wigström (Heirs of Maurice Sandoz Collection, Musée de l'Horlogerie, Le Locle, Switzerland)

27 The Alexander III Equestrian Egg. Dated 1910, signed Fabergé (Armoury Museum, the Kremlin, Moscow) (See also Pl. 125)

28 The Orange Tree Egg. Dated 1911. Signed Fabergé. (The Forbes Collection, New York) (See also Pl. 139)

29 The Napoleonic Egg. Dated 1912. Workmaster H. Wigström (M.G. Gray Foundation Collection, New Orleans) (See also Pl. 132)

30 The Winter Egg. Dated 1913. Lost (See also Pl. 130)

31 The Grisaille Egg. Dated 1914. Workmaster H. Wigström (M.M. Post Collection: the Hillwood Collection, Washington, D.C.) (See also Pl. 134)

32 The Red Cross Egg with Portraits. Dated 1915. Workmaster H. Wigström (L.T. Pratt Collection: Virginia Museum of Fine Arts, Richmond)

33 The Cross of St. George Egg. Dated 1916. Signed Fabergé (The Forbes Collection, New York)

Presented by Tsar Nicholas II to his wife, Alexandra Feodorovna:

35 The Rosebud Egg. Probably presented to Tsarina Alexandra Feodorovna. Said to have been dated 1895. Lost

36 The Egg with Revolving Miniatures. Probable date 1896. Workmaster M. Perchin (L.T. Pratt Collection: Virginia Museum of Fine Arts, Richmond)

37 The Coronation Coach Egg. Dated 1897. Workmaster M. Perchin (The Forbes Collection, New York) (See also Pl. 126)

39 The Madonna-lily Egg. Dated 1899. Workmaster M. Perchin (Armoury Museum, the Kremlin, Moscow) (See also Pl. 127)

40 The Transsiberian Railway Egg. Probably 1900. Workmaster M. Perchin (Armoury Museum, the Kremlin, Moscow)

42 The Clover Egg. Probably presented to Tsarina Alexandra Feodorovna. Dated (?) 1902. Workmaster M. Perchin (Armoury Museum, the Kremlin, Moscow) (See also Pl. 128)

43 The Peter the Great Egg. Probably presented to Tsarina Alexandra Feodorovna. Dated 1903. Workmaster M. Perchin (L. T. Pratt Collection: Virginia Museum of Fine Arts, Richmond) (See also Pl. 133)

44 The Uspensky Cathedral Egg. Dated 1904. Signed Fabergé (Armoury Museum, the Kremlin, Moscow) (See also Pl. 123)

45 The Colonnade Egg. Probable date 1905. Workmaster H. Wigström (Collection of Her Majesty the Queen) (See also Pl. 129)

46 The Swan Egg. Possibly presented to Tsarina Alexandra Feodorovna. Dated 1906 (Heirs of Maurice Sandoz Collection, Musée de l'Horlogerie, Le Locle, Switzerland) (See also Pl. 138)

47 The Rose Trellis Egg. Possibly presented to Tsarina Alexandra Feodorovna. Dated 1907 (The Walters Art Gallery, Baltimore)

48 The Alexander Palace Egg. Dated 1908. Workmaster H. Wigström (Armoury Museum, the Kremlin, Moscow)

49 The Standart Egg. Possibly presented to Tsarina Alexandra Feodorovna. Probable date 1909. Workmaster H. Wigström (Armoury Museum, the Kremlin, Moscow) (See also Pl. 135)

50 The Love Trophy Egg. Probable date 1910 (private collection, U.S.A.)

51 The 15th Anniversary Egg. Dated 1911. Signed Fabergé (The Forbes Collection, New York)

52 The Tsarevitch Egg. Dated 1912. Workmaster H. Wigström (L.T. Pratt Collection: Virginia Museum of Fine Arts, Richmond)

53 The Romanov Tercentenary Egg. Dated 1913. Workmaster H. Wigström (Armoury Museum, the Kremlin, Moscow) (See also Pl. 121)

54 The Mosaic Egg. Dated 1914 (Collection of Her Majesty the Queen) (See also Pl. 136)

55 The Red Cross Egg with Resurrection Triptych. Dated 1915. Work-

master H. Wigström (I. E. Minshall Collection, The Cleveland Museum of Art, Cleveland)

56 The Steel Military Egg. Dated 1916. Workmaster H. Wigström (Armoury Museum, the Kremlin, Moscow)

57 The Twilight Egg. Possibly presented to Tsarina Alexandra Feodorovna. Dated 1917. Workmaster H. Wigström (Fritz Attinger, Zurich) [According to Eugène Fabergé, there was also a wooden egg produced the same year.]

The Kelch Eggs

58 The Hen Egg. Dated 1898. Workmaster M. Perchin (The Forbes Collection, New York) (See also Pl. 141)

59 The Twelve-panel Egg. Dated 1899. Workmaster M. Perchin (Collection of Her Majesty the Queen)

60 The Pine Cone Egg. Dated 1900. Workmaster M. Perchin (private collection, U.S.A.) (See also Pl. 141)

61 The Apple Blossom Egg. Probable date 1901. Workmaster M. Perchin (private collection, U.S.A.) (See also Pl. 141)

62 The Rocaille Egg. Dated 1902. Workmaster M. Perchin (private collection, U.S.A.) (See also Pl. 141)

63 The Bonbonnière Egg. Dated 1903. Workmaster M. Perchin (private collection, U.S.A.) (See also Pl. 141)

64 The Chanticleer Egg. Probable date 1904. Workmaster M. Perchin (The Forbes Collection, New York) (See also Pls. 141 and 143)

Other Eggs

65 The Nicholas II Equestrian Egg. Probably presented by Tsarina Alexandra Feodorovna to her husband, Tsar Nicholas II. Dated 1913. Workmaster V. Aarne (private collection, U.S.A.)

66 The Diamond Trellis Egg. Possibly presented to Tsarina Marie Feodorovna by her husband, Tsar Alexander III. Possible date 1892. Workmaster August Holström (private collection, England)

67 The Youssoupov Easter Egg. Dated 1907. Signed Fabergé (Heirs of Maurice Sandoz Collection, Musée de l'Horlogerie, Le Locle, Switzerland) (See also Pl. 140)

68 The Duchess of Marlborough Egg. Dated 1902. Workmaster M. Perchin (The Forbes Collection, New York) (See also Pl. 142)

69 The Nobel Ice Egg. Date 1914/6. Lost (See also Pl. 141)

1   1884?

2   1885/6

3   1886/7

4

5   1888

6   1889?

7   1890?

8   1891?

9   1892?

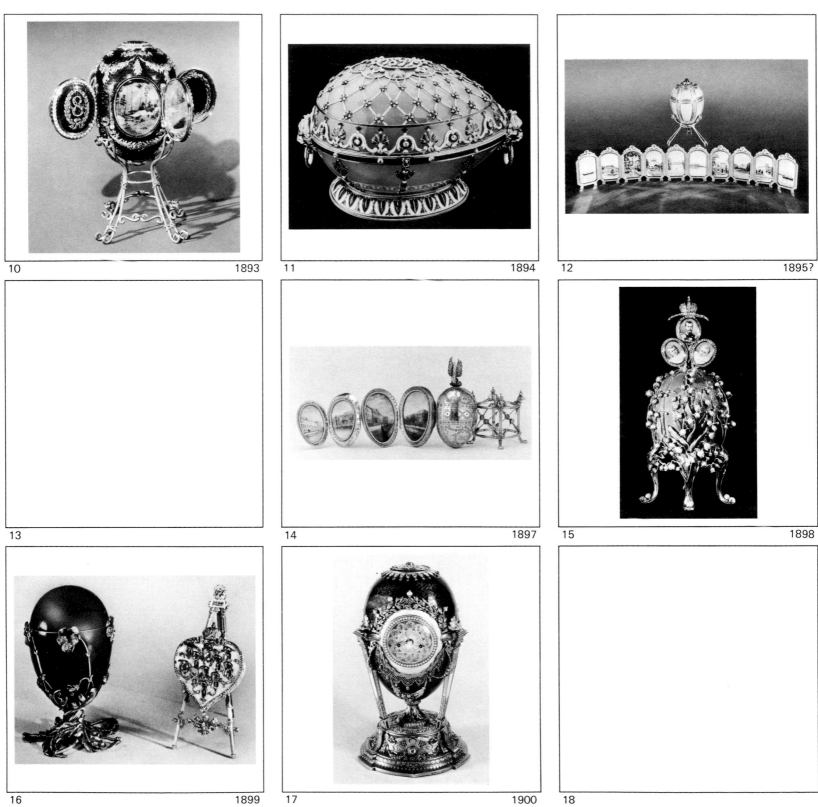

10   1893   11   1894   12   1895?

13   14   1897   15   1898

16   1899   17   1900   18

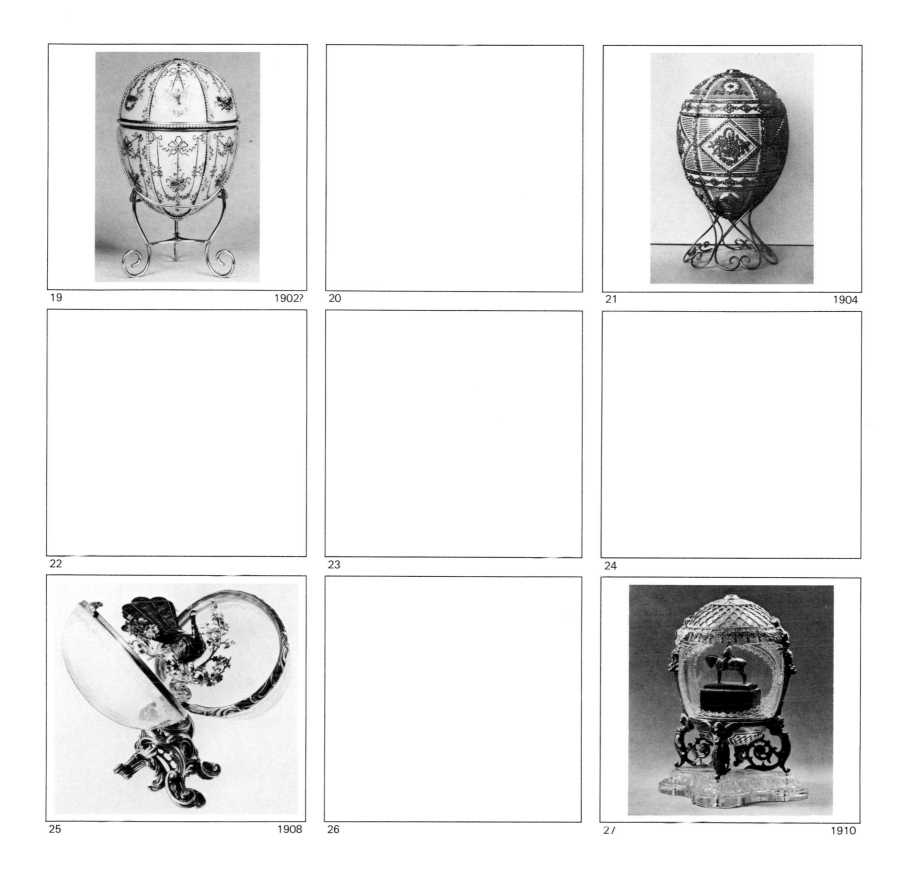

19   1902?

20

21   1904

22

23

24

25   1908

26

27   1910

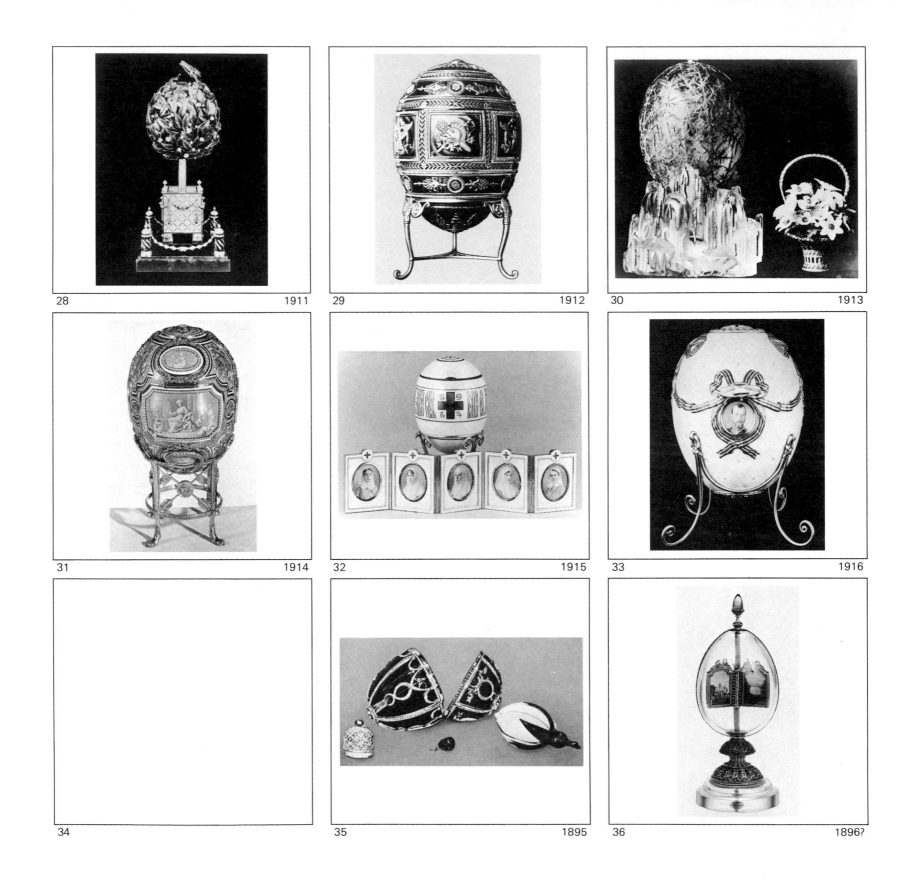

28   1911   29   1912   30   1913

31   1914   32   1915   33   1916

34   35   1895   36   1896?

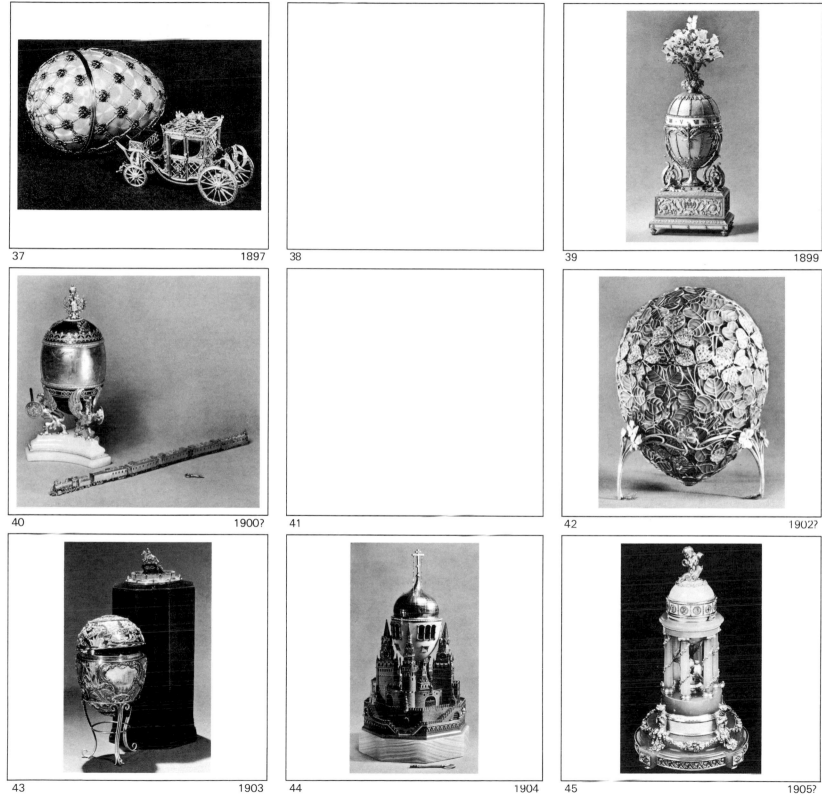

37   1897   38   39   1899

40   1900?   41   42   1902?

43   1903   44   1904   45   1905?

46   1906   47   1907   48   1908

49   1909?   50   1910?   51   1911

52   1912   53   1913   54   1914

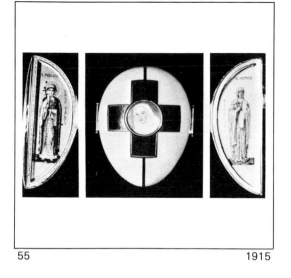

55   1915

56   1916

57   1917

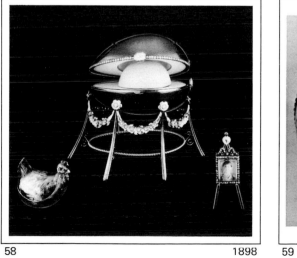

58   1898

59   1899

60   1900

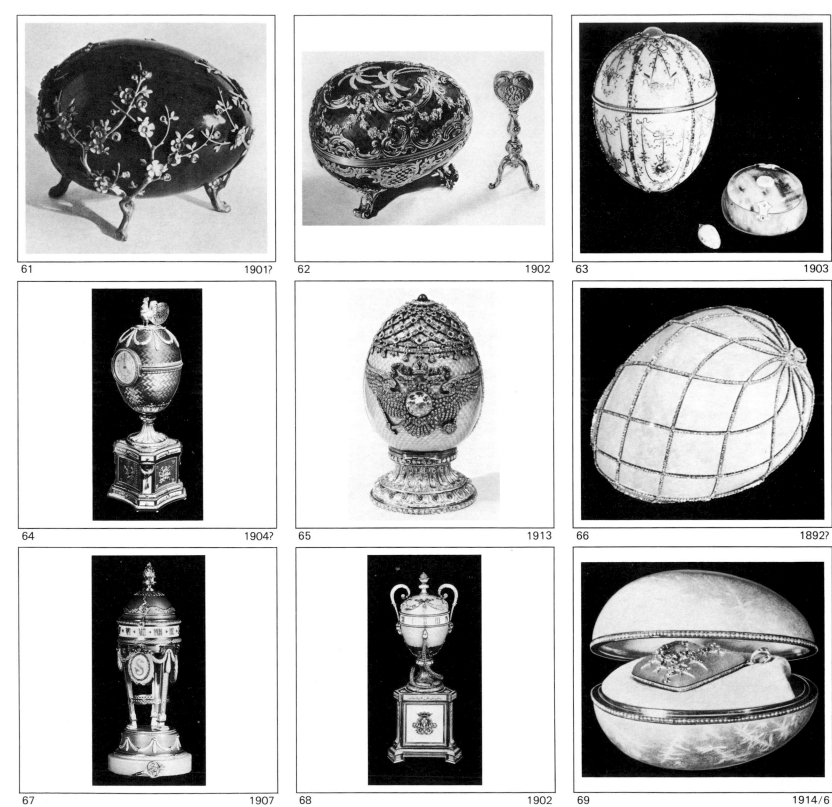

61   1901?

62   1902

63   1903

64   1904?

65   1913

66   1892?

67   1907

68   1902

69   1914/6

Bibliography

I Monographs

1 Bainbridge, H.C. *Peter Carl Fabergé.* London, 1949. reprinted 1966, 1974.
2 Snowman, A.K. *The Art of Carl Fabergé.* London, 1953, 2nd ed. 1962, reprinted 1974.

II Collections

3 Foelkersam, A. von. *Description of the Silver Objects at the Court of His Imperial Majesty* (in Russian). St. Petersburg, 1907.
4 Grady, S. and Fagaly, W.A. *Treasures by Peter Carl Fabergé and Other Master Jewellers: The Matilda Geddings Gray Foundation Collection.* New Orleans Museum of Art, New Orleans, 1972.
5 Hawley, H. *Fabergé and His Contemporaries: The India Early Minshall Collection of the Cleveland Museum of Art.* Cleveland, Ohio, 1967.
6 Lesley, P. *Fabergé: A Catalogue of the Lillian Thomas Pratt Collection of Russian Imperial Jewels.* Virginia Museum of Fine Arts, Richmond, 1976.
7 Rodimtseva, I.A. *Goldsmith Work by the Firms of Fabergé* (in Russian). The Armoury Museum, the Kremlin, Moscow, 1971.
8 Ross, M.C. *Fabergé.* The Walters Art Gallery, Baltimore, Maryland, 1952.
9 *The Art of Carl Fabergé and His Contemporaries.* (M.M. Post Collection), Oklahoma, 1965.
10 Snowman, A.K. *The Lansdell Christie Collection.* The Corcoran Gallery, Washington, D.C., n.d.
11 Waterfield, H. *Fabergé.* The Forbes Magazine Collection, New York, n.d.
12 Waterfield, H. and Forbes, C. *Fabergé: Imperial Easter Eggs and Other Fantasies.* New York, 1978; London, 1979.

III Articles

13 Bainbridge, H.C. 'Russian Imperial Easter Gifts: The Work of Carl Fabergé' in *The Connoisseur* (May/June, 1934), pp. 299–348.
14 'The Workmasters of Fabergé' in *The Connoisseur.* (August, 1935), pp. 87 ff.
15 Berniakovitch, Z.A. 'Goldsmith-work by the Firm of Fabergé' (in Russian) in *Bulletin of the Hermitage.* XXXVIII (Leningrad, 1974), pp. 81 ff.
16 Chanteclair, R. 'La bijouterie étrangère à l'Exposition de 1900' in *Revue de la bijouterie, joaillerie et orfèvrerie.* no. 6 (October, 1900), pp. 61 ff.
17 Guth, P. 'Le Benvenuto Cellini des temps modernes, Carl Fabergé' in *Connaissance des Art.* no. 24 (February, 1954), pp. 40 ff.
18 Habsburg, G. von. 'Carl Fabergé' in *DU Europäische Kunstzeitschrift.* no. 442 (December, 1977).
19 Houillon, L. 'Les émaux à l'Exposition de 1900' in *Revue de la bijouterie, joaillerie et orfèvrerie.* no. 7 (November, 1900), pp. 98 ff.
20 Maingot, E. 'Un orfèvre inoubliable, d'inoubliables créations: Carl Fabergé et ses œufs de Pâques joaillerie' in *Revue française des bijoutiers horlogers.* no. 310 (August, 1966), pp. 78 ff.

21 McNab Dennis, J. 'Fabergé's Objects of Fantasy' in *The Metropolitan Museum of Art Bulletin.* N.S. 23 (New York, 1964–5), pp. 229 ff.
22 Snowman, A.K. 'The Works of Carl Fabergé: The English Royal Collection at Sandringham House; Norfolk' in *The Connoisseur.* (June, 1955), p. 3.
23 'A Group of Virtuoso Pieces by Carl Fabergé and an Easter Egg in the Collection of. H.M. the Queen' in *The Connoisseur.* (June, 1962), pp. 96 ff.
24 'Something about Jewellery' (in Russian) in *Stolitsa i Usadba.* no. 2 (15 January, 1914), pp. 13 f.
25 'Easter Eggs—Presents of the Tsar to Tsarina Alexandra Feodorovna' (in Russian) in *Stolitsa i Usadba.* no. 55 (11 April, 1916), pp. 3 ff.
26 'Fabergé and the Woolcombe-Boyce Collection' in *The Connoisseur.* (June, 1961), pp. 15 ff.

IV Exhibitions

27 *Catalogue of the Exhibition of Russian Art.* 1 Belgrave Square, London, 1935.
28 *Fabergé: His Works.* Hammer Galleries, New York, 1937.
29 *Presentation of Imperial Russian Easter Gifts by Carl Fabergé.* Hammer Galleries, New York, 1939.
30 *A Loan Exhibition of the Works of Carl Fabergé.* Wartski, London, 1949.
31 *Peter Carl Fabergé: An Exhibition of His Works.* A la Vieille Russie, New York, 1949.
32 *Loan Exhibition of the Art of Peter Carl Fabergé.* Hammer Galleries, New York, 1951.
33 *Carl Fabergé: Wartski Coronation Exhibition.* Wartski, London, 1953.
34 *The Art of Peter Carl Fabergé.* A la Vieille Russie, New York, 1961.
35 *The Art of the Goldsmith and the Jeweller.* A la Vieille Russie, New York, 1968.
36 *Fabergé at Wartski: The Famous Group of Ten Russian Figures.* Wartski, London, 1973.
37 *Applied Arts from the Late 19th to Early 20th Century.* The Hermitage, Leningrad, 1974.
38 *Objects of Fantasy: Peter Carl Fabergé and Other Master Jewellers.* National Geographic Institute, Washington, D.C., 1977.
39 *Fabergé, 1846–1920: Goldsmith to the Imperial Court of Russia.* Victoria and Albert Museum, London, 1977.

V General Literature (Marks and Signatures)

40 Bäcksbacka, L. *St. Petersburg Jewellers, Gold- and Silversmiths, 1714–1870* (in Swedish). Helsingfors, 1951.
41 Goldberg, T. a.o. *Russian Gold- and Silversmith Works* (in Russian). Moscow, 1967.
42 Postnikova-Loseva, M.M. *Russian Goldsmith Works, Their Centres and Masters, 16th to 19th Century* (in Russian). Moscow, 1974.

Acknowledgements for Photographs

Reproduced by the gracious permission of Her Majesty the Queen: 81, 93, 94, 102, 105–108, 113c, 116, 129, 136, 151, cat. 54, 59, and the dust jacket

The Armoury Museum, the Kremlin, Moscow: 125, 127, 128

Christie's, London: 103, 109–111

Christie's, Geneva: 19, 21–42, 44, 45, 47–49, 51–56, 58–78, 82–86, 88–92, 95–99, 104, 115, 124, 145, 146, 148, 149, 152, 161–166, 168, 169, 171–175, cat. 57, 65

The Fabergé Family, Geneva: 1, 4, 118–122, 130, 135, 157–159, cat. 5, 8, 21, 27, 30, 39, 40, 42, 44, 48, 49, 53

The Forbes Collection, New York: 126, 137, 139, 142, 143, 147, 150, 167, cat. 1, 7, 11, 15, 28, 33, 37, 51, 58, 64, 68

The Matilda Geddings Grey Foundation, New Orleans: 112, 132, cat. 10, 12, 29

Léon Grinberg, 'A la Vieille Russie', Paris: 18, 43, 57, 141, 160

The Metropolitan Museum of Art, New York: 117

The India Early Minshall Collection, The Cleveland Museum of Art, Cleveland: cat. 55

The Marjorie Merriweather Post Collection, Hillwood, Washington, D.C.: 134, cat. 9, 47

The Lillian Thomas Pratt Collection, The Virginia Museum of Fine Arts, Richmond, Virginia: 133, cat. 14, 32, 36, 43, 52

The Heirs of Maurice Sandoz, Switzerland: 140, 138, cat. 25, 46, 67

Peter Schaffer, 'A la Vieille Russie', New York: 46, 156

A. Kenneth Snowman, Wartski's, London: 2, 3, 5–17, 87, 113b, 144, cat. 6, 66

Mr and Mrs Bernard Solomon, Los Angeles: 13

The Walters Art Gallery, Baltimore: 131, cat. 19, 47

The Wernher Collection, Luton Hoo: 155

Mrs Josianne Woolf: 113a

Index

This book was printed in August, 1979 by Imprimeries Réunies, Lausanne,
who are also responsible for the photolithography.
The setting was furnished by Febel AG, Basle.
The binding is the work of Mayer & Soutter S.A., Renens.
Editorial: Barbara Perroud-Benson.
Design and production: Marcel Berger.

Printed in Switzerland